CREATING EXCELLENCE IN PRIMARY SCHOOL PLAYTIMES

of related interest

How to Get Kids Offline, Outdoors,
and Connecting with Nature
200+ Creative activities to encourage
self-esteem, mindfulness, and wellbeing
Bonnie Thomas
ISBN 978 1 84905 968 8
eISBN 978 0 85700 853 4

Sandtray Play and Storymaking
A Hands-On Approach to Build Academic,
Social, and Emotional Skills in Mainstream
and Special Education
Sheila Dorothy Smith
ISBN 978 1 84905 205 4
eISBN 978 0 85700 436 9

CREATING EXCELLENCE
IN PRIMARY SCHOOL PLAYTIMES

HOW TO MAKE 20% OF THE
SCHOOL DAY 100% BETTER

Michael Follett

Jessica Kingsley *Publishers*
London and Philadelphia

First published in 2017
by Jessica Kingsley Publishers
73 Collier Street
London N1 9BE, UK
and
400 Market Street, Suite 400
Philadelphia, PA 19106, USA

www.jkp.com

Library of Congress Cataloging in Publication Data
A CIP catalog record for this book is available from the Library of Congress

British Library Cataloguing in Publication Data
A CIP catalogue record for this book is available from the British Library

ISBN 978 1 78592 098 1
eISBN 978 1 78450 361 1

Printed and bound in Great Britain

CONTENTS

INTRODUCTION

This book is for anyone involved with schools for children aged between 4 and 12 years who would like to improve the quality of experience for every child, every day. It is based on 20 years of action research working with schools of every size, location and environment, and motivated by respect for the UN Convention on the Rights of the Child, Article 31 (on the right to play) and a belief that it is perfectly possible and beneficial for all schools and pupils, for every child in every school, to have an amazing playtime every day.

It is hard to capture the feeling of walking around a playground at lunchtimes in a school that has become a great provider of play. The sound is different, the atmosphere is different, the children and the adults look different, and slowly a big smile comes on your face as you realise that there is something really special going on. Hundreds of children are having the most basic needs of childhood met, not just today, but every day, every single day of their school lives. It is hard to grasp what it is that's different... You see a 4-year-old playing with 7- and 11-year-olds, a couple of girls building dens with some boys, a group dressed up and performing a dance routine, a huddle of children talking intently about the contents of a saucepan. Then you look round and realise that every single child is engaged in their play, hundreds of bright, enquiring minds and energetic bodies are all finding their own challenges, building their own worlds and directing their own actions. And you wonder why doesn't every school playground look like this?

The scenes above are what I increasingly saw between 2005 and 2011 in the schools I supported in South Gloucestershire.

The programme developed as a result my position in the only post as full-time school improvement officer for play in the UK. During a six-year period around 75 schools took part in a process of action research and development, resulting in a programme that is founded on the principles of the playwork sector, but delivered through the processes and structures of school improvement. Since 2011, Outdoor Play and Learning Community Interest Company (OPAL CIC) has been a social enterprise dedicated to bringing the benefits of a strategic approach to play development in schools to as many children as possible.

This book falls into two parts. The first deals with the background ideas and cultural conditions underlying decision making around play. This is because it is only when a school approaches play development with a clear and consistent value-based approach that it has any chance of creating meaningful and lasting change.

The first chapter explores the background to the question of what play is, and the second chapter is about why play is important. In a climate in which education policy bases success on qualifications children will need in their 20s, we need to take a step away and ask, 'What is it that children need right now for their happiness, their physical, social and mental wellbeing and their development. I have worked with many schools that have spent a lot of time and money on equipment and staff training without having underpinned what they are doing with a firm foundation of agreement about the nature of play and its value. This leads to contradictions in adults' behaviour, money spent on projects with low play value and an emphasis on adult control, direction and outcomes.

Chapter 3 explores the question, 'Why us?' I have been asked many times about why schools should take on every aspect of society's duty to raise children. Do we really have to add play to the long list of wider child-raising duties expected of schools? The chapter shows that even from purely self-interested motives, there are excellent reasons for schools to put time, effort and resources into providing high-quality play.

Chapter 4 looks at the limitations of what is available to schools to address children's play. There is lots of money to be made from schools and no shortage of products aimed at the schools market. Some are well worthwhile but many provide no more than a few minutes passing interest and are then redundant. As an adviser I have to learn to be diplomatic when viewing a new £25,000 structure in a school knowing that the equivalent play value could have been achieved for £25, so to save time and money I have included my opinions and observations about what doesn't work.

Chapter 5 continues on the theme but on a more positive note... What does work well? Again it is based on observations and many hundreds of hours spent in school playgrounds and it covers the types of practical approaches and investments that are likely to engage lots of children for long periods of time.

Chapter 6 is about leadership, the central idea being that an area of school life that takes up the most difficult and challenging 20 per cent of time needs leading from the top, needs ongoing leadership and clear lines of responsibility and communication. Without these, decision making will be determined by fear, impulsive reaction and poor information.

Chapter 7 covers the single area that has such an impact on the ability of children to access the play experiences they need so much...risk. Misunderstanding of the application of 'health and safety' concerns has damaged childhood beyond recognition and is threatening the competence and safety of young adults. The chapter sets out the steps for a sensible, balanced approach to managing both the risks and the benefits of challenge in play.

Chapter 8 is all about building good foundations. I have been involved in writing about play development at every level from national to regional to individual schools. In the end, what every decision comes down to are the values and principles agreed by a group. Without agreement and communication about what we are all trying to achieve, and how we think we can best do it, we are just left with a group of individuals, all with different ideas, motivations and tolerances, reacting to a daily barrage of demands, complaints, arguments and accidents. This is no path to excellence. On the other hand, consistency, inspiration, vision, persistence and innovation all come from a starting point of commonly agreed values, which underpin all good policy.

Chapter 9 challenges the traditional role of the adults who are around during children's playtime and suggests that the role of policing to stop accidents and bad behaviour has a negative impact on play and on the self-image of those asked to fill that role. I suggest that the answer has been hiding in plain sight for many years within the playwork sector. Here there are skills and practices built up over many years, all based on the nuanced application of playwork values, in a field where adults are trying to find the best way of supporting a process that is, to the greatest extent possible, best owned, managed and directed by children.

Chapter 10 is all about our duty as adults to uphold the rights of the child. I do not believe anyone working in a school deliberately sets out to deny children the right to play. But as I visit schools that ban running, or touching or access to nature, or contact between older and younger, or I see play environments that are deserts of grey or green monotony, beset by rotas and prohibitions, I think that every school must take responsibility for the legal and moral obligations behind every child's right to play.

Chapter 11 closes Part I on the cultural conditions for play. It covers the simple principle of use what you have before you invest further in play. The schools I visit vary enormously in the amount of space available. For those with little space, ingenuity is required, like in a well-designed camper van, and for those lucky enough to have space, a commitment to appreciate, value and use an almost priceless asset is required.

Part II moves on to more practical ideas on the layout and resourcing of school play environments. Chapter 12 introduces the concept of the play landscape as a place where children's play ranges across the entire environment, encountering variety and difference and many ways to become engaged with each other and with their surroundings.

Chapter 13 covers the first of the four main principles, the idea of social space. I like to give the example of what would happen if you put a kitten down in the middle of a playground. What would it do? Where would it go? It would probably bolt for the nearest cover. We all feel more comfortable resting, imagining and socialising when we have some sort of enclosure around us. In a school with lots and lots of people, lots of places with at least a sense of protection and enclosure will be needed.

Chapter 14 discusses the second of the four main design principles. It describes the idea of a journey being the way that children link one social space to another, both in the physical sense of their movement and in the way they create movement and narrative in their play. By integrating physical challenge right across a landscape, journeys become a completely natural way of mastering different types of physical movement and a stimulus for the narrative of the play itself.

Chapter 15 introduces the third design principle, the idea of affordance, best summed up, I think, by the understanding that we as adults don't have to know what everything is for in play; we just need to provide variety, quantity and above all difference. In a world filled with so many natural and man-made materials to explore, so many plants and types of earth and minerals and wood and textures, in a three-dimensional existence, and to young beings primed with rapidly developing brains fed by a super-tuned set of senses and boundless curiosity, why would we give children sterile, flat, primary coloured rubber and tarmac deserts to feed their development?

Chapter 16 saves possibly the most important design principle until last. One idea underpinning all play is that of the child as the agent of their own actions, with the ability to change and influence the world around them. They therefore need play environments packed throughout with opportunities for change and influence. In my experience a fixed and unchangeable play environment is one that invites poor behaviour, conflict and destruction, as these are other ways that children find to create an impact on the world around them.

I have specialised in working with schools to improve the quality of play for every child at every playtime for the past 15 years. In writing this book I have drawn on my experiences as playworker, teacher, special needs supporter and local authority school improvement adviser, and above all in developing and delivering the OPAL Outdoor Play and Learning (OPAL) Primary Programme in over 200 schools. My work has taken me all over the UK, to Scandinavia, the USA, Canada, New Zealand and Australia, and while school systems may differ, I believe that all children have the same universal need to play for their wellbeing, happiness and development, and so I hope that the contents of the book will also be relevant beyond the UK.

I have written this book because, while the activity of play is mostly fun, the function of play is serious, and the loss of play from childhood is even more serious. It seems to me just common sense that if we can make our schools perform better, improve children's well-being and health, and solve most behaviour problems, all within the limitations of the spaces and time we already have and for very modest investment, the question should not be 'Why would we?' but 'Why wouldn't we make the effort to make play in every school amazing?'

It seems a great shame that England, which has been in the forefront of so much innovation about play support and development, is so lacking in any current social or educational policy to support children in their right to play, or to realise that great play delivers so many of the outcomes that we want for children today. Children cannot wait for us; they have current needs and their childhoods may have come and gone by the time national policy delivers priorities based on what a child needs from childhood. If every school adopted a well-thought-out strategic approach to delivering high-quality play opportunities for all of their children, no child would have to miss out. I hope that this book inspires and empowers all decision makers connected to education in any way, to make the absolute most of whatever their current situation is and also of the power they hold to ensure every child has an amazing playtime every day, with no exceptions!

— I —

BACKGROUND, THEORY AND SCHOOL CULTURE

1

WHAT IS PLAY AND WHY IS IT IMPORTANT?

It should be easy to define something that every one of us has in common and that was part of our daily lives for many years of our childhood. And yet if you ask a group of adults to define what makes play...play, they struggle to capture its essence. The most commonly used words are 'fun' and 'imagination', closely followed by 'friendship' and 'activity'. But these are certainly not unique to play as they describe what happens when you play but don't define what it is. By describing what it is not we can get closer to a definition: play is different from work, it does not follow set rules like sport and we can't be forced to play, so whatever our age we might say, 'Play is what I do when everyone else has stopped telling me what to do.'[1] What this definition captures is the notion of personal choice and direction, so that in play, conditions allow children to be in charge of themselves.

The playwork sector in the UK is guided by three simple principles which capture the definitive aspects of play. They are that play is:

- self-directed
- intrinsically motivated
- freely chosen.

Self-direction

If we imagine the child as film director, then they are in charge of the story, the props and the action, but they are not working to a script and the plot is open to constant redirection and improvisation. To add complexity, in most of their productions children are not sole directors; they come into contact with other children, each of whom is directing themselves, resulting in an evolving improvised co-production. Those players with a stronger will, more powers of persuasion and/or a clearer vision may well take control of some of the direction, depending on the extent to which the other players choose to give up their self-direction in order to be able to maintain the advantages of playing within the group.

As well as suggesting the idea of being the creator of your own plot, self-direction implies movement towards somewhere: a goal or destination. In some play the direction may be obvious to adults because we can see the outcome, such as the digging of a deep hole or the building of a den, but this is often not the case and adults struggle to see the point of what children are doing in their play, because the direction is constantly shifting and changing or is entirely internal and obscure. This leads adults to make comments like, 'I want their play to be more focused', or 'productive' or 'meaningful'.

When adults enter a play environment they can find it incredibly hard not to intervene with their own direction. This may well be because they have an objective in mind. They want children to playfully reach a predetermined learning objective or want to point out learning or benefit opportunities from the play that is happening. In doing so they have moved what is happening away from being play. It is therefore important for adults to be very self-aware of the consequence of their presence and their actions on the play process. Intervention in direction may well be justified for all kinds of reasons, such as safety or socialisation, but it will have a cost of returning control of direction back to the adult. The very presence of adults in the play environment will have an impact on the play – as in particle physics, the very act of observation alters what is observed. Decisions about intervention should therefore be made with clear reasons and intended outcomes; the more interventions there are, the less likely it is that the activity will continue to be play. Playwork calls this approach 'low intervention – high response'. It requires a self-consciousness from the adult, so that they are not constantly present and influencing play, but when they see the need for intervention they do it consciously and effectively. Finally, they should be aware of the point as soon as possible where they are returning control of direction to the children.

Intrinsic motivation

Intrinsic motivation to play is present in all children. It is what makes a baby want to crawl and then walk, or a child on a shopping trip want to touch and pick up everything they see. We may have to try to motivate children in formal lessons or PE, but the instinct to playfully explore the world is an innate part of human make-up. Children may not be able to verbalise or even know why they are playing in the way they are, but this does not make their actions any less valid. On the other hand, they often have their own reasons for following a particular direction in their play, which may remain known only to them. The experiences they create through their play may be motivated in response to a thought, the environment, a social encounter or a feeling. It may be, like the cavorting of spring lambs, an irrepressible urge just to move, express or feel.

Children are motivated from birth to constantly push at the boundaries of what is already known and already easily accomplished. Play is an evolutionarily driven process, with the most intelligent species, including primates, canines and dolphins, all having play as a significant mechanism for development of intelligence. When children act in ways that we struggle with as adults, by hurting each other or themselves, breaking things, being selfish or rude, they are following their natural drive to explore all of the boundaries around them. All experience is subjective. We cannot tell children what things look like, feel like, sound like, and far less can we tell them what their relationship between their senses and the world is going to be like. They must gather their own data or, as the military would say, their own 'intelligence'. Children are intrinsically motivated to gather experience; some will be pleasant, some unpleasant, some will be 'fun' and some will not, but all experience is relevant. Experience that is gathered because of your own direction, interest or action is the most useful and most relevant to your future learning and development.

Free choice

Freedom of choice is an essential element of play: freedom to choose when you play, where, who with, how long and what with. In a school environment no child will be able to experience total freedom. Play only happens at playtimes, it only happens in the school grounds and in prescribed areas of those grounds. However, the principle of freedom of choice should be one of the strongest principles guiding adults in their decision making about play. Whenever possible, the presumption should be towards enabling choice. For this reason it is a good idea only to use rotas for a maximum of six weeks' transition period of phased change. After six weeks children will find their own balanced level of use across an environment that has sufficient choices available.

From the many schools in the OPAL programme it has universally been found that it is best to let children decide the age of the children they want to play with, and to fully integrate all ages at playtimes across the school. With both access to activities and areas of the playground, the guiding principles should be on the combination of richness of choice and freedom of choice, because real freedom requires options. One head teacher admitted to an OPAL mentor, 'We are very good on equality, everyone has free choice – there is just nothing to choose from.'

Play as the creation of experience

The development of intelligence is a cyclical process working in three stages, which are the same as the cycle described as the play cycle in playwork theory (see Figure 1.1).

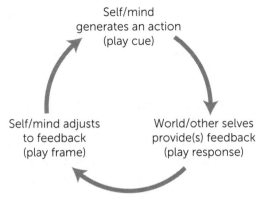

Figure 1.1 Play and learning cycle

The cue

The child generates a 'cue'. This is the creation of some kind of experience, which may be in any realm of experience. These realms of experience can be categorised into personal, environmental, social and cultural. A cue might be a jump, making a face, shouting a new word, breaking a stick, in fact any creative process by the child at all.

The response

In 'the cue' the child was the creative agent of a new prompt to the external world. The world echoes or responds to the child's cue, the jolt of the jump, the smile back at the face, the snap of the stick. The child has created and the world has responded. Like a bat navigating by imperceptible sounds, the child receives constant feedback.

The frame

The frame is the creation of a new piece of understanding. The child may not have gained a full understanding or theory but is able either to create a new category of experience or to fit the response into an existing category. 'When I land on grass it feels soft, when I smile at Jan, Jan smiles back, when I bend dry wood it snaps.' As the bat uses the returning sound waves to precisely locate themselves, so the child uses the response from their cues to build up an understanding of the world that is relevant to them.

The play and intelligence cycle is at the root of building our theoretical understanding of the world and also building and strengthening new physical neural connections in the brain. At the moment the child makes a new frame of understanding as a result of their creative process, a neural pathway is connected in the brain. The value of the process is based on the child as the agent creating the experience. Without this agency it is like a computer appearing to be clever because it has good preset software as opposed to the 'artificial intelligence' of machines that can create their own experiences, create artificial neural networks and apply their learning in future situations. My definition of play from this perspective is 'spontaneously generated social, cultural, physical and internal experience whose purpose is to gain reaction to agency'.

Zones of agency

Figure 1.2 represents the different areas of a child's life in which they have the power to be agents of their own creative experience. Each of the four zones of agency should be thought of as overlapping bubbles. If these spheres are very small, the potential contained within them will be very limited. Our duty as adults is to make these spheres as large as possible, so that although we don't know exactly what children will do, we know that there is as great a potential as possible.

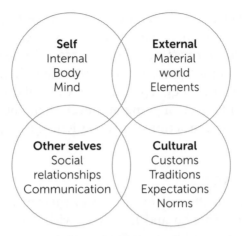

Figure 1.2 Zones of agency

The self

The first area in children's development is the discovery of the self and the boundaries between self and not self. In putting their fists in their mouths babies gradually discover that they are the ones controlling this event and so find out that they are not just passive recipients of sensory information but can influence and control their existence. Throughout childhood – as their bodies, minds and capabilities change – children need constantly to create their own experiences to gauge: What can my body do? What do I look like? What do I think? Play in the areas of exploration of the one's self can be entirely internal; it may involve a spoken narrative about what is happening and will certainly include acting out different behaviours to see what they feel like.

The external material world

Children do not live in isolated bodies; they live in a world full of dimensions, senses, textures, materials and objects. Access to a rich material environment is essential in order to be able to build understanding of what the world is made of and how one relates to it. The patterns of children's exploration of the relationship between themselves and the material world are known as 'schema' and include *rotation, trajectory, enveloping, orientation, positioning, connection, enclosure/containing, transporting* and *transformation*. These schematic behaviours are not just about coming to a static understanding of the nature of the material world, they represent the way children act in that world to maintain an ongoing and ever-changing relationship with it, based on the actions and experiences they generate.

The social world

Children are not the sole occupants of their world. They must learn how to relate to and negotiate with others. Play is the means by which children carry out practical experimentation in the skills and methods of social interaction and behaviour. As with the sphere of the material world, the sphere of potential social interaction should be as large and varied as possible. It is only by having the possibility of social play with children of other ages, gender, background and ability that children will discover what works, who they get on with and how to become socialised. Only play gives children the freedom to try out the successes and failures of a huge range of social skills, competencies and tools.

The cultural world

There are cultural rules and expectations governing all aspects of our behaviour and relations. What is acceptable in one situation is not acceptable in another. For example, wearing your slippers and pyjamas is culturally accepted around the house but not on the school run. Children need and want to explore what are the norms and what happens when you turn them on their head. Their play environments should be places where aspects of children's home culture can be explored and other people's cultures encountered and played with.

Play as culture

Play is the culture of children. It contains all aspects of human creativity, art and inventiveness. It has its own traditions, special places, myths and agreed beliefs. In imaginary play, especially, children create their own worlds, roles, rules, items of higher value, histories and all the other complexities of culture that adults develop. A society of children, playing in a well-resourced environment over a long period of time, reruns the anthropological patterns of development from the past, from the invention of means to make a mark (see the case study below) to the progress from barter to systems of money. In playground observations OPAL mentors have seen plastic beads leaked from bean bags, pebbles, conkers and pine cones all used as currencies in school playgrounds.

When the supervision of play is handed to adults who do not understand what they are seeing and are instructed to supervise play within the narrowest restrictions of 'clean and safe', children's carefully and thoughtfully constructed cultures, in which they invest their time, emotions, ambitions and curiosity, are frequently and repeatedly ignored, undervalued or prohibited. The value of staff whose first instinct in their management of play is to listen, watch and understand is essential if an adult version of cultural imperialism is to be avoided.

CASE STUDY: THE INVENTION OF PAINT

I was watching a group of boys make powder from grinding a brick, a stone and cement on top of a low flag-topped wall. The activity had developed from observing the colour of one powder they had produced themselves to wondering if other powders from other materials would make other colours. They were then adding drops of water to make coloured pastes (a similar activity and observation must have preceded the painting of the caves at Lascaux 10,000 years ago). The boys wanted to share their discoveries, they were excited and proud and so they called over a lunchtime supervisor to see. She talked over their enthusiastic descriptions and abruptly ended the activity with the words, 'Put those stones down. Stones are dangerous and dirty.' I thought, 'What a good job it was we didn't have lunchtime supervisors at the dawn of the Stone Age.' If only the supervisor had been able to appreciate the culture that the group were developing in inventing the basic tools for art and mark making and encouraged further discoveries.

The most important sentence in human development could well be 'I have an idea', because without our ability to create new thoughts that did not exist before, where would we be? We are a species of ideas makers, innovators and inventors. From thin air we create ideas for such things as songs, art, language, stories, poetry, buildings and machines. Where do we get this amazing and very human skill from? It is no coincidence that 'I have an idea' is heard so much in play. 'I have an idea... Let's play dinosaurs...', 'Let's build a bus...', 'Let's pretend we are dragons...', 'Let's invent new rude words...', 'Let's build a den'. Play is not letting off steam. It is not what children do between the important things adults direct them to do. It is the way they learn all of the things that adults can't teach them, and to cap it all its fun too.

KEY POINTS

» Play is child-led behaviour.

» Play is a cyclical process, not an activity or a set of activities.

» Play is the culture of children.

2

WHERE HAS PLAY GONE AND WHY?

Play as wildlife

The existence of play in childhood has much in parallel with the survival of wildlife. 'Without habitat, there is no wildlife. It's that simple' is a slogan of Wildlife Canada. Play, like wildlife, needs certain necessary conditions to exist and thrive, and when these conditions diminish or disappear, then so does the possibility of play. There is a growing consensus, which includes the United Nations (UN), the International Play Association (IPA), groups such as Global Play Advocates, respected writers such as Sue Palmer and Richard Louvre, that rich and varied play opportunities – especially social outdoor play – are disappearing from childhood in many developed and developing countries.

Just as the disappearance of most species is not due to the malicious pursuit of them but to the destruction of their habitats, so play is disappearing not because of nasty adults trying to stamp it out but because the simple conditions for its existence are diminishing. These are time, space, children and permission.

Time

That play requires time sounds too obvious to state, but children's time is under pressure as the demands to be productive and take part in worthwhile outcome-focused activity increase. Screen time for 5–10-year-olds now takes up around four-and-a-half hours a day[2] in the UK and primary school homework one hour.[3]

This is compared to four hours a week outdoor play.[4] Only half of 11-year-olds[5] get to take part in active outdoor play five times a week and 10 per cent of children never play out. Within the school day, time for play in school is becoming less and less over time, with afternoon play having virtually disappeared for 9–11-year-olds, and the pressure of managing the dining hall means that playtime is often reduced from around 65 minutes, as it was in the 1990s, to 30 minutes in a significant number of the schools OPAL works with.[6]

Children enter into different levels of engagement in their play. Short-burst play activities are mainly physical, while complex role-playing, deep imagination and ongoing enquiry into the nature of materials or joint enterprises will require more time to develop and may need to pass through a boredom threshold as a precursor to self-initiated behaviours. The edges of school playtimes are frequently eroded by the adults in charge, so an hour's playtime may well involve ten minutes waiting to eat, ten minutes eating, ten minutes waiting for everyone else to be ready to go out, twenty minutes playing, five minutes tidy-up time and five minutes line-up time. At the extreme, OPAL mentors have found lunchtime supervisors blowing the whistle for tidy-up time twenty minutes before the end of playtime, and playtime is so dull that children themselves queue up during playtime to be let back into class.

Playtime is a valuable resource in a child's life, especially for the play-poor current generation, more so than any in the past. Like preserving a forest rather than patches of woodland, it is the generosity of resource that has value. As other pressures on children's time mount up, the only remaining forest of play is constantly chopped and trimmed away until only tiny vestiges remain.

Space

The second prerequisite for play is space. Where does social outdoor play happen in the life of a modern child? Rising land values have meant that virtually all undeveloped spaces in urban and suburban environments that used to be accessed by children for their play have been developed, cleaned up or made inaccessible. And bomb sites and urban wasteland are largely a thing of the past. Most school grounds, which used to have out-of-school time public access, have been fenced in and so lie unused around 95 per cent of the time. However, all schools have some space for play. Some have vast fields, with woodland and hedges, and some have small areas of tarmac, but even if it is small, for at least 10 per cent of school children it will be the only space they access for their play, and for 50 per cent it will be the only one they access for play five times a week, and so it may be a poor habitat, but it is a habitat.

Children

Some play may be solitary, but most play is social, and nobody really knows how to play as well as other children. Their ability to rapidly alternate between the everyday, real, material and fantasy worlds, and to fully live in the moments of both, sets them aside from adults, who at best can manage suspended disbelief and acted role-play but can never be fully immersed in play. One of the great advantages of play in schools is that there is large pool of fellow players who are available immediately and play may happen if the other habitat conditions are also present.

Permission

Who are the stewards of play? Who notices or cares about the quality of childhood? Who are the gatekeepers who hold the keys to playfulness? The answer to all of these questions is every adult who consciously or unconsciously uses their power in decision making that impacts on play. Adults' inability to see how their decisions erode the possibility of play are responsible like poor stewards of the environment. As children, like sparrows, have quietly disappeared from the public realm, so adult intolerance of the rough edges of children's playfulness has grown and the restrictions of ever-growing prohibitions have tightened on the freedoms that give breath to play. Every school in the UK has three out of four of the habitat conditions for play. They all have time, spaces and children, but permission is the vital cultural condition and without it the others are meaningless. What use are fields if you are not allowed to get dirty, or bushes if you must remain in adult view at all time, or friendship where touching is banned, or equipment if you can only go around it clockwise on the third Tuesday in June, watched over by an adult? In every school that OPAL has worked with it is the culture of permissions that is the most significant factor in either poverty of play opportunities or its scope for improvement.

Fear is not a policy

To an almost universal extent, a 'culture of fear' has become the main policy driver for schools in relation to play. This is exacerbated by an absence of any counteracting philosophy concerning play and reflects a similar media-fuelled fear-driven approach to policy in wider society. Policy gives consistent and value-based reason to future decisions. Both reason and fear begin with the question, 'What if?'. The difference is that with reason there is balance and proportionality. When fear takes control without the opportunity for calm and reasoned assessment of the risks, benefits and proportionality of the response, the result will be that fear trumps everything, because the attitude prevails that if there is a risk, however small, and there is a solution, however expensive, then protection wins. So, for example, a small village primary school, with no history of stranger danger, abductions or 'escapees', will spend thousands of pounds on prison-style security fencing and electronic access. A reasoned approach should counterbalance the fear-based view and argue that historically there has never been a security problem on the site, and that feeding a diet of fear to children about their community is itself damaging. Additionally, the thousands of pounds spent could be invested in the quality of the play and learning environment, which has many well-evidenced benefits. Reason should win but, because fear plays the trump card in raising strong emotions, often it does not.

The range of sources of fear for schools are numerous and include OFSTED, parents, the media, health and safety inspectors, insurers, litigation, gossip, social media and the local authority.

Without a robust philosophy of childhood and clearly expressed beliefs in the role of the school as an institution of child development, rather than a test-processing mechanism, schools are at the mercy of the most fearful in their community to dictate their policies. The most fearful parent, the over-zealous caretaker, the most frightened supervisor and the most officious and ill-informed health and safety inspector are at present the most influential policy determiners for childhood in our schools.

The word education comes from the Latin *educo*, 'I lead'. But in what direction are schools leading? OPAL's experience of working in around 200 schools suggests that the culture of fear in schools is leading parents and children away from a model of a positive and playful childhood, where children are encouraged to be independent, capable and competent. Instead it is leading towards models of childhood where every minute is timetabled and purposed by someone else, every idea directed, every outcome predetermined, every risk eliminated and every fear magnified.

We must be aware that children learn all of the time from everything they experience. So what are they really learning in school?

- In isolating and fortifying schools from their communities, children are learning to be fearful of being outside in public spaces beyond school, and of the people in their communities.

- In being afraid of letting children play in all weathers, children are learning that we live in a country where the weather is not suitable to be outside for much of the year and it is better to remain safely indoors, in front of a screen.

- In our fear of children playing beyond the sightline of adults, children are learning that they are not trustworthy and do not have the ability to self-regulate.

- In our fear of them getting their clothes or themselves dirty, children are learning to fear the natural environment and to prioritise appearance beyond experience.

- In denying all physical risk and over-recording the smallest of hurts, children are learning to be attention seeking, weak and lacking in resilience.

- In our fear of parental complaints and accusations of bullying, children are learning that they are not capable of complex social interactions without the constant interventions of an adult.

Allowing fear to dictate policy rarely produces wise or well-informed results. Without ethos how is decision making to be ethical?

It is beyond the remit of this book to suggest how the education system as a whole could or should be changed. We are left with the reality of play having been driven out of all areas of children's lives, including their education, in most developed and developing nations and we face the question of whether we want to do anything about it right now for the children in our schools today.

KEY POINTS

» The habitat of play is disappearing.

» Society has changed but children's needs have not.

» Up to 50 per cent of primary school children only play outside at school.

3

WHY SHOULD SCHOOLS IMPROVE PLAY?

Despite playtimes being shortened, children still spend around 20 per cent of their school time in playtimes (see Figure 3.1). This can be thought about in different ways. It is equivalent to one day a week of school, or during the seven years at primary school it will be 1.2 to 1.4 years of a child's primary school life. When considered like this it seems extraordinary that play is not thought of as part of a school's core business and that it does not have agreed beliefs and values informing its improvements.

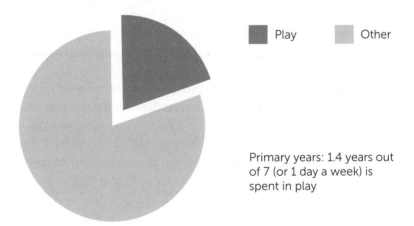

Primary years: 1.4 years out of 7 (or 1 day a week) is spent in play

Figure 3.1 Play makes up 20 per cent of school life in UK primary schools

In many schools the people supervising play are on the minimum wage, they are employed for the minimum time, with minimum management and little or no budget. Is it any wonder so many schools find playtimes hard to manage and improvements hard to sustain?

Another approach is to think about child play hours. For every hundred children in a school there are about 20,000 child play hours spent per year. A village primary school will therefore have around 22,000 child play hours per year, a two-form-entry town school of 350 pupils around 70,000 hours and an urban school of 550 pupils 110,000 child play hours a year. Who manages the resources and staffing of this time? If education is leadership, then where is the plan and what are the beliefs so that this amount of time is meeting the needs of children whose outdoor play opportunities beyond school are so diminished?

The costs of poor play

The impact of poor playtimes on schools varies widely. In some schools playtimes do not appear to be the cause of many problems; in others they are the single source of the majority of behaviour incidents and can take up the valuable and costly time of many adults. In a large school the head or senior management team (SMT) may be regularly dealing with incidents, and teachers will be spending 5 to 15 minutes of post-lunchtime lessons resolving issues, teaching assistants will be diverted from teaching support to post-playtime behaviour support and lunchtime staff will be spending their efforts on conflict and argument firefighting instead of positive playwork intervention. OPAL's research suggests that when the full cost of adults' time is added up, a two-form-entry primary school of around 260 children can be spending between £4000 and £5500 a year on the negative outcomes of poor playtimes. Schools that have effectively and sustainably addressed play report an 80–90 per cent reduction in these costs. The value to schools of a 90 per cent reduction in head or SMT time taken in playtime issue resolution also has benefits to leadership going far beyond the monetary savings.

The capital value of outside space

A lack of understanding of what play is, and the kind of landscapes and environments that best diversify and enrich play lead to an assumption that improvement can be made through spending more on play equipment. The first priority should always to be exploit the value of what the school already has, and land is the most valuable asset a school will ever own. Some schools have huge amounts of space, others have almost none, and virtually all could use what they have more effectively.

> **CASE STUDY:** USING WHAT YOU ALREADY OWN
>
> A primary school in the West Country had allocated £20,000 to improve the quality of the Early Years outdoor play environment. Following an advisory visit it emerged that a beautiful area of completely unused ornamental land at the front of the school could be incorporated into the Early Years area at a cost of around £9000 for moving the fence. Based on local property prices the value of the land was around £120,000. The newly accessed land had established trees, grass and hedges that would have taken years to mature and provided a ready-made new environment.

Land value and use of assets

Many suburban primary schools are lucky enough to have playing fields in what have now become much more built-up areas. Access to open green space is one of the most important elements of play environments, so access to playing fields has considerable value, which should be quantified by the current cost to acquire the land. Even a modest village school playing field would have a value of hundreds of thousands of pounds, suburban schools of millions and urban schools tens of millions. If schools want to improve play, then acknowledging existing asset value and accessing these spaces should be seen as an absolute priority.

Accessed land by area

Children love to play in all sorts of different kinds of spaces, large and small, open and enclosed, artificial and natural. Their nature is to explore and come to understand geography by playing in it. It is often possible to increase the amount of space that can be accessed once the school has reviewed its ideas of models of supervision and appropriate clothing and footware.

CASE STUDY: RECLAIMING SPACE FOR PLAY

I was asked to help in an infant school that had a lot of collisions at playtime and where the head teacher spent every lunchtime supervising play because behaviour had deteriorated and the supervisors were increasingly relying on 'benefit removal' (see page 62) to control play. I found that the bramble hedge on the edge of the playground was four metres deep. We had it cut back and added $100m^2$ to the playground. The unchallenging play equipment was old and too slippery, and the remaining equipment was not used in the wet. We removed the oldest equipment and changed the policy on access to the rubber surface and added $80m^2$. The end of the school was fenced off as delivery lorries had to access the site once a day. We moved the fence and banned deliveries at lunchtimes, adding $225m^2$. The border of one side of the playground was large shrubs at the top of a small bank. Lots of signs told children to keep off the bank and out of the bushes. We replaced them with signs that said, 'Please play on the bank and in the bushes', adding another $240m^2$. The 'quiet nature garden' was almost never used, so we allowed the oldest two year groups access during playtimes, after replacing the pond with a sand pit, adding a further $200m^2$. The grassy areas were out of bounds most of the year. After some footwear policy changes, we accessed them all year, adding a further $450m^2$. The area around the sides and back of the storage shed had been 'out of bounds'. This was made 'in bounds', adding another $35m^2$. The reception class had their own area which was the only link between the two narrow strips of tarmac playground. This was opened up for all at playtimes, adding 75m².

We had started with 500m² of tarmac and added 1400m² of reclaimed playable space. All of the reclaimed space was much more interesting and varied to play in than the tarmac. The total cost was around £1800, just over £1 per square metre. The land value if bought would have been £200–£300 a square metre, coming in at a total of £350,000.

The result was a 95 per cent drop in behaviour problems at playtimes.

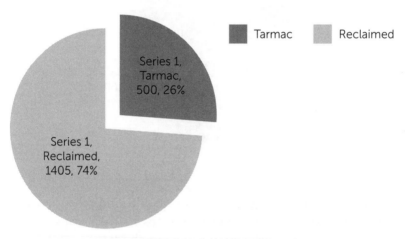

Figure 3.2 Land reclaimed for play

Land accessed by time

It is important to remember that 50 per cent of UK children only play outside with friends during the school day,[7] so being able to access field spaces is crucial to their physical and mental wellbeing. When asking staff about use of the field, there is one phrase that comes up in almost every visit. The answer to 'Do you use the field for play?' is 'Yes, in the summer term' or 'Yes, in the good weather'. When asked what percentage of the available days per year they would access the field, most schools will say 'around 50–60 per cent'.

Breaking down the figures gives a surprisingly different figure. There are 180 school days in the year broken into six terms of around 30 days per term. If schools use the field in the summer term, what they mean is days in the summer term when it hasn't just rained, isn't raining or doesn't look like it will probably rain. Met Office figures show that in a British summer it will rain on one in three days. This brings the figure down to an average of 20 days per year when the field is judged to be dry enough to play on.

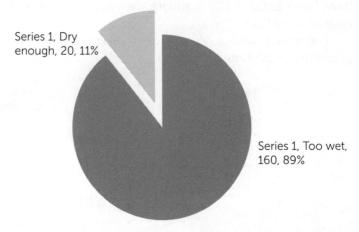

Figure 3.3 Average playing field use

The percentages in Figure 3.3 are reversible, and schools which have adopted significant policy changes in their approach to clothing, footwear, dirt, supervision and children's competence in being able to make sensible judgements for themselves are able to allow access to their fields for around 90 per cent of the year. The remaining 10 per cent is when it is too wet to go out even with appropriate clothing.

The degree of access to the outdoors in all weather is almost entirely cultural. British schools may keep children in if there has been snow or a heavy frost. Guidelines in Canada say that children should be kept in if temperatures drop below –29 degrees Celsius and schools in Sweden have one compulsory day's outside teaching a week. Britain is a temperate, rainy and muddy country. The job of schools should be to equip children with the appropriate dress, attitudes and skills to live in their home climate and not to think that the outdoors is unsuitable for use 89 per cent of the time.

United Nations Convention on the Rights of the Child, Article 31

Since 1992 it has been the legal duty of the UK government to implement the UN Convention on the Rights of the Child (UNCRC). The convention is made up of 54 Articles. Among them is Article 31 (Leisure, play and culture): 'Children have the right to relax and play, and to join in a wide range of cultural, artistic and other recreational activities.'[8]

In 2013 the United Nations published General comment 17 on children's right to play. Its purpose was to reprimand the developed nations for their inaction in implementing Article 31, stating that based on 'its reviews of implementation of the rights of the child under the Convention [the Committee] is concerned by the poor recognition given by States to Article 31 rights.'[9]

The General comment says that a significant reason for the lack of implementation across governments and institutions is due to 'Lack of awareness of the importance of play and recreation: In many parts of the world, play is perceived as "deficit" time spent in frivolous or unproductive activity of no intrinsic worth' (p.11).

The UN holds a strong view that schools have a legal and moral human rights obligation to ensure that all children in their care have good access to high-quality play opportunities. The duty of schools under the convention is set out below.[10]

> **Schools**: Educational environments should play a major role in fulfilling the obligations under article 31, including:
>
> - *Physical environment of settings*: States parties should aim to ensure the provision of adequate indoor and outdoor space to facilitate play, sports, games and drama, during and around school hours; active promotion of equal opportunities for both girls and boys to play; adequate sanitation facilities for boys and girls; playgrounds, play landscapes and equipment that are safe and properly and regularly inspected; playgrounds with appropriate boundaries; equipment

and spaces designed to enable all children, including children with disabilities, to participate equally; play areas which afford opportunities for all forms of play; location and design of play areas with adequate protection and with the involvement of children in the design and development;

- *Structure of the day*: Statutory provision, including homework, should guarantee appropriate time during the day to ensure that children have sufficient opportunity for rest and play, in accordance with their age and developmental needs;

- *School curriculum*: Consistent with obligations under article 29 concerning the aims of education, appropriate time and expertise must be allocated within the school curriculum for children to learn, participate in and generate cultural and artistic activities, including music, drama, literature, poetry and art, as well as sports and games;

- *Educational pedagogy*: Learning environments should be active and participatory and offer, especially in the early years, playful activities and forms of engagement.

Play is a universal right for all children regardless of their age, sex, gender or ability, and given that all countries, bar the USA, have made the UNCRC legally binding, all schools should be providing leadership to parents and society in implementation of the convention. If the UN has also thought it necessary to state in a General comment that schools must play their part in implementation, and that failure to appreciate the importance of play in the child's life and the school day is an international problem, there can be no justification for schools not having a strategic approach to play founded on sound pedagogy and human rights and rooted in a school's own clear policy.

KEY POINTS

» Play makes up 20 per cent of school life.

» Schools hugely underuse and undervalue land assets.

» Play provision is a legal and moral human rights obligation.

— 4 —

THE LIMITATIONS OF EXISTING SOLUTIONS

Introduction

The market for play equipment and other play services to schools has grown steadily and after a brief pause around 2010 now seems to be growing again. Every year schools spend millions of pounds on changes to the play environment with trim-trails (a series of low-level outdoor play equipment often arranged in an arc or circle), play equipment, playground markings, playground musical instruments, outdoor classrooms, planting and landscape. They also invest in training courses for lunchtime staff in activities such as skipping workshops and traditional playground games.

CASE STUDY: LEARNING THE HARD WAY

During my time as Play Officer for Bath and North East Somerset, before I developed OPAL, I provided training for around 70 per cent of the authority's lunchtime play staff on traditional playground games. It involved around six hours of training and included a resource file of many games. To my dismay I discovered that about six weeks after the end of the course I had made almost no difference to the quality of play in the schools. I think this was partly because the games were an adult-initiated and directed activity and depended on ongoing adult input, which soon waned. Also it was a mistake to think that the supervisors had enough of a stake in the school to be able to support long-lasting change without a wider programme supporting play improvement and greater valuing of their role.

There is something about money raised for play projects in primary schools that creates a sense of urgency to spend it. The school may not have raised any money for play for years but once it is there it creates its own sense of urgency that it needs to be spent. Not only this but if the parents have been involved in the fundraising it needs to have been seen to be spent. This distorts judgements about priorities for the spending. Visibility, size and even colour become criteria that may be elevated above more child-centred considerations such as function, play, longevity and practicality.

In a school in the South East, the parents had raised the funds and chosen three large wooden features which took up around one quarter of the available play space. The features were made of round pressure-treated wood and set on a blue rubber 'safety surface'. When I visited the school several years after the equipment had been installed, the area with the equipment in it was regularly closed off if the wood was wet. In the British climate there are very few weeks when it is either not raining or has not recently rained. The reason given for the closure was that both the wood and the rubber get too slippery to use in the wet. At the school there was a severe problem with physical overcrowding, and the loss of a large area of the playground owing to a safety surface that made the area less safe seemed ironic. In the end we decided that any equipment that could not be use in the wet would either be treated so that it could be used or would be removed.

The lessons from this school include:

- In a school where space is at a premium, don't sacrifice large amounts of it to features that only a few children will use for part of the year.

- We live in a country with lots of rain. Both wood and rubber get very slippery in frost and rain, so think carefully about how much space you sacrifice to surfaces that may be unusable in the British climate.

- Rubber safety surfaces do not prevent accidents or injury; they reduce the chance of serious head trauma in cases of falls from a height onto the head.

Most primary schools now have some kind of playground equipment. It has often been funded by the parents–teachers association (PTA) and chosen from a catalogue or website. The most common choice for primary schools is the trim-trail or adventure-trail.

The use of trim-trails tends to follow a similar pattern over the year. In September it is crowded with reception and early years children, in October it's less crowded, by December it is often used by a handful of children, and for much of the rest of the year it is often no more than a very expensive seat. Observations in the USA, New Zealand, Germany, Denmark and Sweden indicate that nowhere else is there such widespread use of this type of outdoor unchallenging play equipment. In these countries they provide a combination of natural play opportunities and full-scale play equipment of the type found in public parks.

The play industry will happily provide any equipment that there is a demand for, and schools buy equipment provided by the play industry because it assumes it must have value if it is being sold. The quality of build and materials with the reputable companies is largely good and so the equipment may last 15 years, but the level of challenge and engagement may well be no more than 15 minutes. Schools must be the ones to question the value of return on the money they invest. The following should be considered when thinking about fixed play equipment.

- Children will have up to seven years playing on the equipment. If the purpose is to offer physical challenge and the challenge can be mastered within the first couple of play sessions, then such unchallenging challenges will render the equipment largely redundant in a very short time.

- If the purpose is to present excitement, there must be an element of risk. Most trim- or adventure-trail equipment is designed with the minimum fall height possible, usually 400mm. This is great from a safety point of view, but the elimination of risk is accompanied by the elimination of excitement, making the equipment redundant and boring after the first couple of uses.

- If the purpose is physical development, then consider what kinds of development are on offer. Most of the low-level equipment provides many variations on the schema of balance, sometimes with a small amount of instability and wobbliness. This kind of offer can as effectively be replicated with a plank and two car tyres. Look for types of physical movement and challenge that cannot easily be provided by simple alternatives, such as hanging upside down, spinning and upper body strength.

- The play equipment is usually installed as a trail, each piece in a line with the next piece. Inevitably children either use pieces at different speeds or more commonly just sit on it, blocking the intended flow and requiring adult intervention, rotas and prescribed flow direction. Play is freely chosen, self-directed and self-motivated. Once adults impose directions, rotas, rules and speeds there is little play opportunity remaining.

- Adults tend to think play in schools is only about physical movement and that playground equipment will therefore be the best way to improve playtime behaviour and the quality of play. Great play may well involve movement, but it also involves creativity, sociability, cooperation, involvement, combination, transportation, engagement, control, affinity to nature, access to natural elements, exploration, investigation, rest, refuge and many more qualities. The nurturing of these qualities is not addressed by the simple trim-trail and is best done by school staff who understand the nature of child development. The play value return on expenditure is likely to be much higher when invested in other types of play.

- Observation of newly installed trim-trails across many schools is that after the initial six weeks, when the newness factor still applies (children will always play on anything new), usage settles down to around 5–8 per cent of the population playing on the equipment for around 5–10 per cent of their playtime. This compares with a figure of around 60 per cent of children playing with loose parts for about 60 per cent of the time.

- Design is important. We know the way our house is designed affects the way we use it; the layout, spaces, connections, distribution of features, flow, congestion, accessibility, materials and aesthetics of a play environment are all relevant to its value and use. There is no evidence to suggest primary-coloured materials and bright rubber surfaces appeal to primary age children, whereas there is much evidence to link access to natural environments to improved attention, health and wellbeing.

- The rubber safer surfacing often installed around the equipment is only 'safer' in that it is designed to reduce the risk of head injury in a fall from height, which is not the kind of fall experienced from low-level trails. It is extremely slippery in the wet and cold, which is the majority of British weather, leading to the new equipment areas being closed for much of the year.

- If rubber surfacing is chosen, only the highest quality should be used, as cheaper products, especially those made from car tyres, have been linked to the release of high levels of harmful volatile organic compounds (VOCs) and leaching of heavy metals.

If trim-trail and adventure-trail types of school playground equipment are so ineffective and offer so little play value return for investment, why does every play company offer them and why do so many schools buy them? Companies offer them for a number of reasons:

- The primary reason is that they make lots of money. The equipment is not offered by child development specialists; it is offered by commercial companies whose first aim is to make money. This is entirely understandable but means the buyer must be informed about pedagogy and play value and not rely on the seller.

- The equipment is relatively simple to design, construct and install, and so companies can offer several separate items instead of one 'big-ticket' item.

- Several lower-cost items will cover a larger area and the play safety surface around the equipment doubles the cost, so the more safety surface needed, the bigger the sale.

- No one wants to see a child get hurt or injured, including the companies that make the equipment, so they prefer to sell super-safe equipment that has virtually no risk. This is appealing to schools, which also don't like to increase the chance of accidents, giving rise to the uniquely British category of unchallenging-challenging play equipment. In other countries, even the litigious US, if equipment is installed it tends to be larger-scale challenging equipment.

- Schools are competitive and want to have what other schools have. As many schools have a trim-trail, most schools feel that they should have one, so the schools create a demand and the companies supply what the schools markets ask for.

- Capital investment in play equipment is often funded by parents through the PTA, which likes to see quantity and visibility in return for their fundraising efforts, resulting in a lot of unchallenging play offers covering a large area, rather than a single item that would present more challenge over time.

The interest of parents can be capitalised on to enable the school to develop a much more informed design brief, which may have surprising results.

> **CASE STUDY:** DIY NATURE PLAY
>
> A married couple, one an occupational therapist and the other a water engineer, got involved in researching companies to install traditional play equipment on behalf of the PTA at their children's school in Perth, Western Australia. Their research led them away from fixed equipment to the idea of play landscapes, incorporating elements of equipment along with a whole landscape approach to play design. They were unable to find a company to do the work, which drew mainly on inspiration from Europe, so they did it themselves. The first project led to another, and then another, and the formation of a company called Nature Play Solutions that now installs play landscapes in playgrounds and public spaces across Western Australia.

Based on many hundreds of observations from schools that took part in the OPAL Primary Programme, the following observations about what doesn't work in relation to fixed play equipment may be useful.

What doesn't work?

Fenced in play equipment

Fencing in play equipment discourages play because it severely limits choices about how children move and incorporate the equipment into their play. At its best, equipment is an interesting stop-off point within a landscape of many features of difference. When fenced, the purpose becomes fixed like the equipment. You go into the assigned area, do the assigned movement and then what?

Playground markings

Playground markings are bright and visible but have short-term novelty appeal with very rapid drop-off in use. Children are attracted to newness and difference for around two to six weeks. Most playground markings older than six weeks seem to become invisible to children.

Too-small spaces

Most playhouses or towers on play equipment are just too small for children to play in, especially if more than two children want to develop an imaginative or role-play game within the space. Ensure structures are big enough to play in as well as get in, and ensure groups as well as pairs of children can fit in the spaces.

Too few and not enough

There are hundreds of children in most playgrounds. Providing a small amount of a resource or one nice space may well increase conflict, not cooperation. Be generous!

Activity boards

Single-function activity boards provide 'seconds of fun' and fall into the 'instant regret' category of equipment.

Climbing walls

Most climbing walls do not lead from anywhere to anywhere and have only a single route of low-level challenge. As a result most are tried, mastered and abandoned in a very short time.

Music boards

Low- and medium-quality music boards, especially when not integrated within a social space, tend to attract a couple of hits and fail to engage children.

Giant playground chess

This is one to avoid. A busy playground is not the place for a game of chess. However, the large pieces are fun loose parts.

Prescribed imagination

A good play environment will be full of difference and potential. Open-ended spaces and a rich diversity of materials are fuel to imagination. In providing prescribed elements such as pirate ships, planes or trains, we are imposing our own limits to their imaginative capabilities. As primary school children are in a school environment for over 180 hours a year for seven years, we should question how much of that time they would really want to be playing pilots, pirates or passengers!

Insufficient challenge

Children are immensely capable and competent and need to challenge and extend the capabilities of their bodies. Early years, infant and junior play environments should enable the most capable, as well as the least capable, to be able to continue to have physically challenging and demanding environments. Sadly, many settings choose equipment aimed at providing a small amount of challenge to the least capable, and so provide very little value for most of their children for most of the time they will be accessing it.

Lack of thought about migration

Loose material will always spill out and travel. Don't put small pebbles near tarmac, sand near drains or stones where they will get into mowers.

KEY POINTS

» Unchallenging play equipment is a waste of money.

» Play improvement requires a whole-school strategic approach.

» Engaging play takes place across a whole enriched landscape.

— 5 —

WHAT WORKS?

Swinging bars: Single or parallel metal bars

Girls love to hang upside down. Boys probably do too but in every playground visited that had metal bars for swinging round, the girls monopolised the equipment. It would therefore be sensible to provide lots of these in an area – so that being around the bars is social and there is less competition to use them – and provide them at different heights to meet the needs of different ages and abilities.

Monkey bars: Hand-over-hand journey hanging from arms

These are difficult and require real strength and coordination. Children will keep returning to them until they have mastered them. At least two levels of height and challenge should ensure use over a prolonged time.

Hangout equipment

Equipment which provides several quite large areas of flat netting at various heights always becomes a popular social hanging out and messing about space.

Playground edge equipment

If there are multiple pieces of equipment they work well when set all down one side of the tarmac. This is because children soon tire of using equipment in series and use it as a social base for their play. The function becomes one of a physical hanging-out space where children chat while also moving their bodies. They also will use the equipment as bases for 'burst–rest' play where they run between bases in short bursts, then hang out on equipment.

Integrated equipment

When equipment is integrated across a landscape its use is also integrated into the imaginary and physical journeys of play. A slide down a bank, a lookout tower on a hill or a bridge between two hills will be encountered and incorporated into the imaginary world children construct in their play rather than being prescribed as a set of physical movements that are meant to take place within this space at this time.

Challenge

Risk aversion in the UK has led to the predominance of low-challenge–low-risk equipment. In the USA, Sweden, Germany, New Zealand and Australia it is common to find play equipment that presents real physical challenge, even for 11- and 12-year-olds, and this continues to be used throughout children's time at school.

Water and sand

As any parent who has taken mixed-age families to the beach knows, there is no age limit to the fascination of sand and water play on a big scale.

Surfacing as play material

Moveable natural material is fuel to many kinds of play. When choosing surfacing remember that moveable materials such as sand, bark chip and pea gravel serve both as impact attenuating surfaces and as a source of play material.

High-quality tuned instruments

Tuned and chromatically scaled steel drums, glockenspiels and tubular bells – but only very good-quality ones – will engage children. They are best placed within a performance or gathering social space.

Marking the playground

For the same cost as permanent playground markings it is possible to buy around 6000 boxes of jumbo chalk. Imaginative play staff can mark up the playground in different ways every day and also ration out boxes of chalk so that children can mark the playground. Markings could include hopscotch, king-ball, story writing, graffiti projects, themed illustration, searches, delivery games, numbers, letters, animals, Pokemon, etc. The key is that the play staff and the children have the ability to create a new play surface and content every day.

Design briefs and grounds planning

The only way for schools to ensure they get an outdoor play landscape that serves their children's needs is for them to carefully create their own design brief. Schools that ask a play equipment company to write their design brief end up being told they need lots of their equipment! A good design brief will be based on an understanding of play, of the current legal support for risk in play and some simple principles of good design. Schools should use their brief to develop a long-term grounds plan or they will end up with lots of randomly placed bits of equipment.

KEY POINTS

» Growing bodies need real challenge.

» Loose surfacing adds safety and play value.

» Thoughtful design really matters.

— 6 —

LEADERSHIP AND THE CULTURE OF PLAY

Why is leadership important?

Organisations cannot have a character but we do refer to them by their characteristics, such as friendly, professional, organised, etc. What we mean is usually based on our emotional response to our experiences of them. A friendly organisation is one where we experienced a friendly response to our encounters with people in the organisation.

The role of the head teacher in a primary school is to provide leadership. Without leadership coherent decision making based on agreed policy is unlikely. Research from over 200 schools that completed the OPAL Primary Programme shows that only around 2 per cent have organised structures for managing and improving the quality of their play. In these, a member of senior leadership plans for the improvement of the quality of play over time, reviews progress and manages play staff and play resources with a view to creating ongoing improvements.

A much more common arrangement is that improvements in the play environment are led in response to capital projects, either external fundraising from parent groups or occasional investment from the school budget. Leadership for these projects in most cases will be by parent groups or by school staff who take on a temporary leadership role until the money is spent.

The results of these temporary leadership roles is extremely mixed because there are rarely principles or values to inform how the money is spent, and the commercial play industry providers become the primary source of expertise and provision, either because the investment is based on what is made available through catalogues, or sales reps are happy to provide design advice to help schools make their choices on how to spend the school's money. The big problem with this approach is one of interests. Strong leadership in play within a school team should be able to decide what best serves the interests of the children by getting the most play value for spend rather than what maximises the play company's sales. However, frequently schools rely on play companies to provide what they think is a good design and as a result the schools spend large amounts of money on attractive-looking items with little lasting value.

Historical leadership in play

Leadership in developing play opportunities in primary schools in the past has been haphazard, sporadic and driven by individual projects to spend some capital or occasionally by a motivated individual leading. When the money is spent or the individual moves on, the motivation for improvement wanes and leadership and direction are lost.

Contradictory values

There is a deep unacknowledged contradiction in primary schools' attitudes to play, one that early years staff are most keenly aware of. It leads to sharp and arbitrary divisions in meeting developmental needs and is a source of tension and unhappiness for many children. The source of the contradiction is that primary education has two very different educational models divided sharply at the move from reception to Year 1. Schools largely acknowledge and value the role of play in developing children's core skills and physical, intellectual and emotional wellbeing – when children are in nursery and their first year of school. Children are encouraged to build their skills in managing their own behaviours, spend as much time as possible outdoors, direct their own enquires and delight in the joy of discovery. What is extraordinary about the UK education system is that when you pass your fifth birthday, the fun times are over. The testing regime approach hits hard and lessons are almost exclusively indoors, and playful learning, delight and self-motivated and driven enquiry become a luxury saved for the occasional special reward.

However, there is a glimmer of hope: a small but significant proportion of the school day that is acknowledged as playtime. This is being continually eroded, and in some secondary schools has disappeared altogether, but all primary schools still have a total of 40 to 75 minutes a day for eating and play. This is 1.4 years of school time that does not have to be dominated by test regimes and adult-driven anxieties about performance. The premise already exists that it is for play, and if it is used effectively, this time could contribute hugely to readdressing the loss of access to social outdoor play out of school and provide playful, self-directed, experiential learning within school.

The opportunity for every child to have an hour of high-quality outdoor social play in an environment enriched for many play types and staffed by adults who are dedicated to providing excellence, and skilled and knowledgeable in playwork, is too good and too important an opportunity to pass up.

In all other areas of school improvement the assumption that a proportion as large as 20 per cent of school life would somehow look after itself if a group of people were employed on minimum wage, with little or no management, no consistent approaches, no values, no recognition, and sporadic and inappropriate investment is unthinkable, and yet in relation to play it is the modus operandi. What has been lacking in the past is thoughtful and consistent senior leadership. When this is in place, then the status and value of play, and the thought and planning to support it, becomes possible.

What happens when there is no leadership?

Improving play in primary schools is an area of school improvement. Schools don't spontaneously create dramatic changes and improvements in practice, certainly not ones that last. Some schools can have periods of improvement led by one or two practitioners, but change dependent on an individual's character and not on replicable roles and widespread support will never create lasting change or improvement.

How do you sustain leadership?

The goal for school improvement is not just to make things better for the term of a project but to make sustainable change for the better permanent. This is not easy. Things have a tendency to slip back if you don't have your eye on them; it is the principle of atrophy. For head teachers it is difficult to be the one who maintains the momentum for improvement all of the time. OPAL has worked in over 200 schools over a period of 16 years. Some schools made some improvements and have now gone back to where they were before. Some made huge improvements and have slipped back but to a better position than before. And some have maintained a huge increase in quality for over ten years. The common factor in the last group is the creation of roles of responsibility for play in the school so that the head teacher is not the only one managing quality, and when an individual leaves the role is passed on and ownership of roles is sustained.

Leadership roles should be created at each tier of decision making – ideally a play advocate on the board or governing body, a play strategy lead on the senior management team (SMT), a curricular or subject lead for play from among the teachers and a play team coordinator managing everyday practice and resources.

Can leadership survive changes of staff?

With this structure in place there is a good chance that management of improved play will survive staff changes, especially if role descriptions are clear and positions are replaced as staff move on. Experience from the schools that have been involved in the OPAL Primary Programme is that without these staffing changes, improvements in play will be a project-based event where quality improves for a limited time and then gradually falls back to where it was before as resources become used up and decision making reverts to benefit withdrawal in response to challenging events.

The importance of consensus and consistency in play

CASE STUDY: HOW OPINIONS BECOME RULES

I was walking around a school in Bristol with the head teacher at lunchtime when we both noticed that children who were playing on the playfield avoided using a 10m strip near the fence. I asked the head, John, why this was but he had no idea, so we stopped a child and asked. 'It's not allowed.' We asked why but the child didn't know, so we stopped another; the response was the same. 'Not allowed but don't know why.' Finally we asked an older Year 6 girl. 'It's because the dinner ladies say we might distract the cars on the roundabout and make them crash.'

We then saw that no children were playing on the bank. Eventually we found out from the children that this was known to be a rule because they might twist and break their ankle. Many schools have similar cultures of prohibition where the origins of the decision have been lost but the rules survive.

This example shows how playground rules expand to fill a vacuum when there are no other values to guide reasoned decision making. In a school where a benefit–risk approach had been adopted and staff are given time to discuss issues about how they can deal with concerns while maximising play benefits, choice and work to playwork principles, the proliferation of prohibition is kept in check.

A second force at work is children's propensity to obey. While we all notice the rule-breakers, the rule-keepers are the unnoticed majority. As they develop, children are always looking for patterns and rules to follow about how life works, what is expected of them, what is acceptable to others and what is not. Unless adults are able to put a check on their rule making, then every time one adult creates a rule based on their opinion, such as not standing on those rocks or not picking up stones, these are added to the ever-growing list of prohibitions.

It is essential that adults discuss and question the implications of the prohibitive culture of playgrounds, as they may have profound and unintended consequences. An example from school policies found on the Internet is: 'No touching, keep hands and feet to yourself'. What kind of message does this rule give to children? How do children and all living sentient beings respond to touch? How important is the expression of ourselves through touch? How important is touch to children's understanding of the world and to their wellbeing? It is deeply disturbing that adults in charge of child development are responsible for such an approach in the name of being responsible, which is only marginally different from the physical restraint of children.

CASE STUDY: THE PRESSURE COOKER EFFECT

The pressure cooker effect describes an existing problem of prohibition compounded by further levels of prohibition to try to resolve an issue but instead leads to a more pressured, problematic environment.

I was asked to help at an infant school where a colleague of mine from the school improvement team had gone to take up headship. Although the children were only ages four to eight, there were more and more problems at playtime. An adviser from another organisation had suggested banning running to 'calm things down' and cut down the number of collision accidents, but the behaviour of the children was getting worse, as was their attitude to the lunchtime staff. It turned out that children were prohibited from using around 60 per cent of available space in the school and so the collisions were being caused by overcrowding, not poor behaviour. I found it truly horrifying that anyone who has observed the developmental behaviours of any species of mammal should contemplate 'not running' as a good idea.

Once the space issues had been resolved and children were allowed to run and exhibit normal child/species behaviours, then the other problems went away.

In the case study above it should have been clear to the adults involved that young children need to run and that the problems of collisions be tackled in other ways. In a benefit–risk assessment we would have to consider the impact on their current health of not running, the impact on their mental health of not doing something all of their instincts are telling them to do, and the impact on their future health of thinking that running is bad. The thought of infants released from the enclosure and restriction of a classroom to a playtime without running should ring alarm bells for any adult who is able to step back from the pressures of finding immediate solutions and consider childhood needs.

The 10m fence rules and the no running rules are examples of immediacy rather than inconsistency. They arise from the need to tackle an issue now, and someone comes up with a prohibitive rule as a solution. If there is a play policy or a set of checks and balances based on values, a prohibitive rule may be assessed to see if its impact is balanced and proportionate and in keeping with the school's values. If not, then a rule may well be consistent but at best pointless and at worst deeply damaging to children's development – for example, no touching.

In many playgrounds the supervisors all make up their own rules and the teachers make up a different set when they are on duty. Common themes for inconsistencies are you are/are not allowed into that space or area, you are/are not allowed to climb on objects or trees, you are/are not allowed to play bulldog/football. This environment is confusing for children, irritating for staff and potentially dangerous, as justified and sensible prohibitions are likely to be ignored as rules seem to have no sense or justification.

A school is like a ship. It is hierarchical not democratic, but requires the confidence and support of all involved. The ship's captain provides the focus of leadership, takes ultimate responsibility and plots the course. Improving play in schools will be led or will founder on the conviction of the head and whether this is a course they want to take or not, as decisions that need to be made about budgets, clothing, risk and resources all come back to them. Once the course is set, then delegation of clear roles is essential if it is to be maintained, and the support and consensus of all others involved must be obtained.

KEY POINTS

» Only clear leadership can steer the direction a school takes.

» Consistency in decision making is essential in managing play.

» Sustainable change only happens when supported by clear leadership roles.

— 7 —

MANAGING RISK

What does it look like?

Managing risk in the playground is much harder than managing risk in the classroom. A good play environment should have potential for all sorts of things to happen, be explored, moved, combined, transported, climbed on, etc. It should be a place of evolving challenge, progressing with ability and time. Learning to cope in this kind of environment can only be achieved through learning what you yourself are capable of. Being safe, or at least safe enough, requires the ability to imagine and predict the probable outcomes of events. When others are present you must be able to negotiate with them on what everyone is comfortable with. If the agreed level of risk is based on the competencies of the least able, the environment is going to be deeply frustrating and restrictive for the development of most children. What is needed is a dynamic approach with vigilant informed staff, and competent and empowered children. There will still be some absolute rules and safeguards necessary to ensure that 'there is not unreasonable risk of death or serious injury'.[11] However, most situations will need ongoing discussion, negotiation and communication as they unfold.

What is children's role in it?

The ultimate responsibility for the safety of children in school lies with the adults in charge, but it is against children's interests to over-protect them and may ultimately endanger them in future. Children should be partners in the processes involved in risk management because they are especially aware of the benefits of their actions.

If an important part of education is to provide children with the skills and knowledge that will help them lead successful, happy and fulfilled lives in the present and in the future, then they must be practised in making their own judgements and dealing with the results of those judgements.

THREE APPROACHES TO CHILDREN'S ROLE IN BENEFIT–RISK MANAGEMENT

Model 1: Benefit removal

The adult spots a potential risk, which is eliminated by removing the entire activity along with any benefits.

EXAMPLE

Children have found some stones of different sizes in the hedge at the edge of the playground and are using them to make miniature pretend houses. A supervisor spots what they are doing and tells them that playing with stones is not allowed because they are dangerous. She moves the children away, then removes the stones so that no one else will be able to play with them.

Model 2: Adult risk reduction

The adult identifies a potential risk and provides a solution so that the benefit can be maintained.

EXAMPLE

A group of children have got some tyres and are stacking them up into a tower and sitting on the top. The activity is on the tarmac. The supervisor spots a potential risk and tells the children that if they want to make tyre towers they must do so on the grass.

Model 3: Child learning

The adult or child identifies a potential risk. The adult supports the child to learn an appropriate way to manage the risk, through identification and actions to reduce the likelihood of harm.

EXAMPLE

A group of children are jumping on a wooden pallet and one section breaks, exposing a nail. The children can see this is a risk and come to ask the supervisor what they should do. The supervisor asks the children to identify the risk and what could be done about it without getting rid of the benefit. In this case the children say the nail could be removed. The supervisor provides some pliers, and the children remove the nail and return to playing with the pallet, which now has a much lower risk.

Background on risk in schools

Schools have felt the need to eliminate risk from the children in their care in response to pressure from all sides: from parents, local authority health and safety officers, insurance inspectors, safety engineers, OFSTED inspectors and the children themselves. In the face of the amount of ill-informed advice abundant in the area of health and safety, they need to be especially informed, supported and encouraged to change their practice.

Schools in the UK are obliged by law to manage risk in two ways. They have a 'duty of care' in civil law to ensure they have acted in a reasonable way to protect the children in their care from harm. Schools are also subject to The Health and Safety at Work Act 1974. The intention of the Act was to protect employees from serious harm and injury in the course of their work. As the Act applied to workplaces it also came to be used for spaces the public had access to, including schools.

The legislation itself says that 'risks should be reduced so far as is reasonably practicable'. This allows for consideration to be taken of other factors apart from the risk of harm.

These may include the cost of managing the risk and whether this is realistic and proportionate to the risk and the inconvenience. It also allows for the concept of having good reasons to take the risk.

Until 2000 interpretation of the Act came to be dominated by the perception that risk should be eliminated from play environments. This led to a culture of myths and misperceptions around health and safety. Real examples resulting from these misperceptions include the ideas that children need to wear protective clothing to play conkers, that if they play with mud it should be 'clean mud', that children cannot play with water that may have any germs in it or that getting a splinter is a serious health and safety concern. These misinterpretations arose because of attempts to manage risk in play as if it was the same as risk in the workplace. For example, in the game of conkers the players take it in turns to try to strike a kind of large nut suspended on a string held by the other player and smash it to win points. One of the risks is getting whacked on the knuckles by your opponent's conker. In a workplace it would make sense to wear protective gloves to avoid any chance of getting hit, but in the game it is part of the excitement and provides an opportunity for children to manage building their resilience by overcoming manageable fears and manageable hurt.

In 2000, a statement on 'Managing Risk in Play' was published by the Play Safety Forum, a national advisory body comprising every major national body connected with children's play and safety, including the Health and Safety Executive, RoSPA and the Local Government Association. The statement has become the foundation for a new approach to managing risk in play and forms the basis for the government-supported document *Managing Risk in Play Provision: Implementation Guide*, first published in 2008 and updated in 2012.[12] The premise of this approach is that taking risks is an essential part of the play process and that there are benefits to children being allowed to experience risks in their play. It also recognises that children must learn eventually to become competent and independent judges of risk themselves if they are to live safe and fulfilling lives in the wider world.

The Managing Risk Key Points position statement says:

Children need and want to take risks when they play. Play provision aims to respond to these needs and wishes by offering children stimulating, challenging environments for exploring and developing their abilities. In doing this, play provision aims to manage the level of risk so that children are not exposed to unacceptable risks of death or serious injury. (p.109)

The importance of this statement in relation to schools' *perception* of risk cannot be overstated. Perceptions of serious injury are hugely exaggerated in schools: grazes, bumps, scratches, bruises and the occasional long limb fracture are thought of as serious injuries, while these are in fact the inevitable consequence of a play environment that meets the play needs of children and are not serious injuries.

In September 2012 the Health and Safety Executive published a four-page guidance document which represents the most significant support for moving away from the benefit-removal model popularised by the Health and Safety Act approach since 1974. It is called 'Children's Play and Leisure: Promoting a Balanced Approach'.[13] The key message is:

Play is great for children's well-being and development. When planning and providing play opportunities, the goal is not to eliminate risk, but to weigh up the risks and benefits. No child will learn about risk if they are wrapped in cotton wool. (p.1)

The document clearly supports a shift from benefit removal to a child-led, learning, risk–benefit approach:

HSE fully recognises that play brings the world to life for children. It provides for an exploration and understanding of their abilities; helps them to learn and develop; and exposes them to the realities of the world in which they will live, which is a world not free from risk but rather one where risk is ever present. The opportunity for play develops a child's risk awareness and prepares them for their future lives. (para.6)

The guidance aims to ensure that schools do not unnecessarily reduce the benefits of play and do not introduce management of risk that is disproportionate, stating that it is important providers' arrangements ensure that:

- the level of risk and challenge in play should not be reduced unnecessarily and the benefits maintained

- risk management decisions do not focus on the petty or fanciful but on real risks

- the controls put in place are proportionate to the degree of risk (see below).

In order to emphasise what a proportionate response means, their main concern is:

- in the design and provision of play opportunities both the risks and the benefits are weighed up

- risks which are not beneficial to the play activity or which are most serious are the focus of control measures

- it is accepted that risk might be introduced as an intentional aspect of a play opportunity

- it is understood that controls should not and cannot aim to eliminate all risk and so even with good management there will always be the possibility of serious life-threatening injuries

- a full range of beneficial play experiences are experienced by children.

In 2012 the Play Safety Forum published the second edition of 'Managing Risk in Play Provision'.[14] This free downloadable resource is essential reading for anyone wanting to understand and implement the child-learning risk–benefit approach. UK schools and all those who advise them about risk should have a good working knowledge of both the H&SE guidance 'Children's Play and Leisure: Promoting a Balanced Approach'[15] and the above-mentioned Play Safety Forum's 'Managing Risk in Play Provision: Implementation Guide' if they are to help schools change their practices. If schools encounter either independent or local government advisers on risk who are not knowledgeable in both of these documents, they are justified in seeking alternative advice from those who are. Schools outside of the UK do not have the benefit of such clear guidance on managing risk in play. However, they may use these documents to put pressure on their national, state or provincial authorities to provide much-needed clear guidance.

Towards a child-learning risk–benefit approach

The first question that needs answering before schools can manage risk is 'What are schools for?' If schools are only for producing children who satisfy the current requirement for national testing and exam results, then management of risk is a simple matter, as all benefit can be removed along with all risk. This makes life clear-cut and simple, as anything judged to be a risk can be banned or removed. Despite increasing pressure from society and government, very few primary schools would place value in adopting such an approach.

If it is agreed that schools are about more than just test results, that they are about preparation for life – the whole child; their mental, physical, social and cultural development and wellbeing – it is absolutely essential for schools to develop a more sophisticated attitude to risk than the benefit-removal model which is so prevalent. The ability to follow a risk–benefit approach can only be made in the context of the school having a play policy and a coherent and strategic approach to play development. It is the historical lack of such an approach that has led to the predominance of the benefit-removal approach.

CASE STUDY: OUT ON A LIMB

Tree climbing is a difficult area of risk–benefit for schools to manage but can be done if a risk-management process is put in place. Following consultation with their children, one of my OPAL schools decided they would allow tree climbing. Firstly the children helped indentify which trees it would be sensible to allow climbing in and which ones would not be. The children recognised that trees near spiked fences were not good ones. The school then had some whole-school assemblies on technique. Their approach was.

- Don't put your weight on anything smaller than your wrist.
- Keep three points of contact with the tree and only move one point at a time.
- No helping other people up.
- Look and test before trusting a branch.
- Keep your body close to the trunk.

The children were able to follow the guidelines they had helped to come up with.

Indentifying your practice

It should be remembered that most schools' practice around play is not deliberate and that it is not the way it is because adults have made a conscious effort to create a culture that inhibits play and stalls development; it has just slowly evolved from many sets of uncoordinated responses to past events and opinions. The first step is to identify what is happening. In many cases senior leadership may have very little idea of what rules the lunchtime supervisors have built up over the years as they are rarely written down and may vary from person to person. In other cases they may be negative rules framed in a positive way.

The benefit-removal model is illustrated by such common practices as:

- No running. We only walk.
- No touching. We keep our hands and feet to ourselves.
- No playing in the bushes. We stay on the playground.
- No playing anywhere out of sight. We can always be seen by an adult.
- No going on grass when it's wet. We can play on the grass when it is dry.

We can reframe these restrictions in light of a benefit-removal approach as follows:

- *Nothing to play with*. Given a good imagination anything moveable could be dangerous and so is removed or not provided.

- *No mixed-age play*. Larger children are dangerous to smaller children and so should also be removed from the environment.

In almost every case the rules will be justified from a risk-prevention perspective. The logic is clear – remove the opportunity and so remove the risk. However, if we term this approach 'benefit removal', it is at least clear and honest what we are doing.

Indentifying risks and hazards

Not every object or situation that presents the opportunity of harm has any or proportionate benefits. In this case we can identify it as a hazard rather than a risk and confidently remove it without having to worry about benefit removal. Some examples of this may be a broken bottle in the grass, a hidden nail sticking out of a plank used for den-building or an exposed electrical wire. These examples all pose different levels of potential harm and no accompanying benefit. It is the duty of adults providing play environments to identify and deal with hazards. Before a play environment is opened for the day a visual check should be made for hazards.

CASE STUDY: COMPETENCE BUILDING

A village primary school I worked with near Durham completely changed their approach to using their huge grounds as part of their play-development strategy. Instead of banning children from the woodland, they got them to identify potential risks. These included some fairly deep, abandoned badgers' set holes. The children painted some of the ply tyres red and they were placed in the woods as risk markers. The children were alerted to the presence of the risk and then expected to manage it themselves. Through continuous involvement and discussion, children at the school are becoming more practised in identifying and manging risk.

Over-protection is as big a threat to children's safety and wellbeing as negligence. It's just we don't get sued for over-protection and we fear being sued for negligence. Only when we temper our fears with our belief in the competence of children, and only if we are motivated by our duty to provide as well as to protect will we be able to make sensible and balanced decisions about risk and challenge in play.

KEY POINTS

» Risk is essential to all development and learning.

» Decisions on risk should always take the benefits into consideration.

» Children should be supported to understand and manage risks with adults support.

8

VALUES AND POLICY

Policy and planning

Why a policy?

A school's identity is defined by its policies and its ability to put them into practice as much as an individual's character can be defined by their values and their ability to act on them. Without guiding principles, the decision making of individuals within institutions is left to chance, the persuasiveness of outsiders, expediency and reaction to crisis. It is important to be able to step back and ask, 'Why do we do that?

Robust group decisions

A play policy is an absolute must for all schools wishing to improve the play opportunities they offer their children. Without one, decision making will not be robust – the response to problems or accidents will be to withdraw, prohibit and diminish. Good decision making weighs up the benefits against the disbenefits and seeks to create a balance, between maintaining maximum benefit whilst managing disbenefits to an acceptable level. Without a play policy the individual is left to come up with their own justifications for a course of actions and this favours an ever-diminishing play offer.

A policy starts with definition and value

A school's play policy needs to begin by answering two questions: what is play, and why is play important in childhood? Unless these questions can be answered in an informed and considered way, all other decisions about play are at risk of being flawed. How can a play environment be equipped and resourced, staff be trained and managed, and difficulties be overcome if there are no agreed principles on the nature and value of the play process? If the nature of play and its vital function in all areas of children's mental, social, cultural and physical wellbeing and development are not agreed, stated, explained and celebrated, how can any individual know what course of action is reasonable for the school to take?

Policy and rights

A play policy should take at its heart the UN Convention on the Rights of the Child, Article 31, and the school's commitment to use its agreed values and principles in all decisions that have an impact on children's access to rich, varied, self-directed play opportunities. A list of actions or a list of prohibitions or directives on certain kinds of behaviour expectations is not a play policy.

Communicating values

Schools should be able to be proud of their values and communicate them effectively to their children, staff and parent communities. Most schools do not do this in relation to play. As a result, their policies are reactive and are in effect set by the two or three parents who complain the most. And so a complaint about a scratch on the arm from the bushes results in the bushes being out of bounds or a complaint about muddy trousers means the field is out of bounds. An apologetic policy on play is not going to drive cultural change. Parents, staff and children need to be involved in the development of an informed consensus about the role of play in child development, in happiness and wellbeing, in a good childhood and in the everyday life of a primary school.

The value of planning

Good planning is the foundation to creating change. It is no coincidence that the word for the future tense is the same as the word for intention. We need to 'will' something and then it 'will happen'. Planning for play should be managed in a strategic and effective way but the content of play itself should not. Schools should have a policy to express their values and principles, a strategy to express their long-term goals and an action plan to map out exactly who will do what and when. Each of these areas of planning should sit within the same framework as other important areas of school planning, so that the policies are updated, the strategies adjusted and the action plans reset. Planning alone does not guarantee improvement; schools are always under many pressures, which means plans may not be carried out: key staff leaving, inspections being announced and child protection issues may all take precedence over play.

The importance of reflection and self-evaluation

The only way to ensure plans are adaptive to circumstances is to make sure a process of reflective practice and self- or external evaluation is applied to play development in the same way it is to other areas of school improvement. A play strategy review process and report should be included in every annual report to governors or the board, and play staff should work to an evaluative cycle based on three points: What are we trying to achieve? How well are we doing it? How can we do it better? These questions should be asked in relation to the values of the play policy and the playwork principles.

Play and target culture

Schools tend to be good at planning, reflective practice, goal setting and evaluation in many areas, but play appears to be an exception. It may be the word that is the problem. It implies frivolity, spontaneity, fluidity and fun. This does not fit with the language of business management that has come to dominate the planning of childhood. Where are the objectives, the goals and the planned outcomes? Can play really be valuable if it is not Specific, Measurable, Achievable, Realistic and Timed (SMART)? The contradictions of play are confusing; how do you plan for the unplanned and direct self-direction?

CASE STUDY: PLAY TEAM BUILDING

At a large primary school on the edge of the Cotswold Hills in Gloucestershire, the job description of supervisor and teaching assistant on lunchtime duty were replaced, so that during playtimes everyone was part of the play team. They were provided with clothes to do their job, which included a branded play team waterproof, fleece liner, t-shirt and a choice of welly boots. They have their own communication board and regular planning and assessment meetings. The time for the job was increased by 15 minutes a day to allow for a five-minute pre-brief and a ten-minute tidy down.

The status of play

Because play is a process and not about production there is a particular need for schools to be able to identify the benefits of the process to their staff and parents. Without intentional messages, only the visible signs of play will communicate the school's approach, and as good play environments are flexible, open ended and child controlled, adults may struggle to see the point of the kind of resources provided and the way they are used.

CASE STUDY: IS IT PLAY?

I went to visit a school that was proud of its trim-trail. This one was made up of a low-level balance beam, some wooden stumps, a wobbly bridge and tyres on chains. The supervisor standing next to the equipment explained that access to it was on a rota. Today was Tuesday so it was Year 2's turn. The equipment despite, being surrounded by £3000 of rubber safety surface extending for a metre in all directions, was only open when it was not frosty or wet. The linear nature of the equipment meant that the supervisor monitored movement to go in one direction and as a queue formed behind encouraged the children to move on. I looked at these children being herded clockwise around these dull obstacles, because it was a dry Tuesday and thought back to my playworker training about play being self-directed, intrinsically motivated and freely chosen and wondered what I was looking at. It bore no resemblance to play.

Communication

Why ongoing communication is especially important in play culture

Managing play is about managing independence, autonomy and transfer of power and decision making. If the meaning of play for the players is self-direction, self-initiation and freedom of choice, and the role of the managers of play is application of rigid rules, minimising any risk and exercising adult control, the relationship is going to be a very difficult and troubled one. It is no wonder that many schools struggle with maintaining motivated and inspirational staff to supervise play, given the impossible remit of the job.

If a school wishes to improve the quality of their play they will need to change the quality of the relationships between adults and children in play. There will have to be discussion, negotiation and respect. Communication will be necessary and sustained between everyone who holds power over play and influences decision making. When OPAL works with schools we set out communication strategies for parents, play staff, teachers, children and other staff. Any one of these groups can derail attempts to change the play ethos. OPAL has examples where in effect the caretaker or the groundsman were the principle dictators of policy, because nobody was brave enough to negotiate with them to change their positions on the purpose of the school grounds. There is a standing joke that schools would run so much more smoothly without children, and some grounds staff view children as a huge obstacle to their work rather than being the reason for the job to exist.

The power relationship between children and adults means that children do not have the power to negotiate their positions and so adults must be able to do this for them. A policy is the foundation for a shift in the power relationship. The policy says that at the highest level of decision making this is what we agree is valuable and important. But a policy is not an instruction manual; it requires interpretation. If you are trying to manage play for 4–11-year-olds on a set of non-negotiable rules, then they will end up being set for the lowest common denominator, because the range of potential between an August birthday reception child and a September birthday Year 6 is huge. One may be barely able to run or climb, the other may achieve more than many adults. A school play environment needs to meet the developmental needs of children who differ vastly in their current and potential abilities.

In addition, play is about a creative process. The outcomes, purpose, content and activities that emerge are created in the flow of a constant cycle of invention, action and communication. The adults in charge of play need to keep up, they need to understand why what is happening is happening, and they need to ensure their intervention allows for the greatest possible potential while staying within the bounds of a 'safe enough' approach. This mental flexibility requires a workplace where people talk to each other. The play team will need to communicate to each other about how they will develop a consistent basis for negotiating with children around a type of play that has emerged. The play team will need to communicate to the teachers about how they are managing emerging play issues, so that there is consistency of approach between morning play and lunchtime supervision. The school will need to communicate with parents to help them understand what their children are doing, why they are doing it, and to create a positive and celebratory dialogue about play rather than the only communication being about negative behaviour issues.

CASE STUDY: CHILDREN AS COMPETENT AND TRUSTWORTHY PEOPLE

I took part in a study tour of schools in Scandinavia run by the play landscape designer Frode Svane. We were in a school in Malmö, Sweden. It was in the middle of a public park and there were no fences separating the school from the park. There was one teacher on lunchtime playtime duty for 250 children, and small groups of children were setting off around the park. I asked the teacher about the rules for how play was managed. She looked at me the way many Scandinavians looked at me when I asked stupid English-person questions on that trip and replied in her talking-to-a-simple-person tone, 'They come and make a negotiation with us.' This was the reply to how almost anything was managed between teacher and pupils.

Communication strategies on play

Children

During a period of cultural change in a school there will need to be very frequent, possibly weekly, play assemblies to celebrate, inform and negotiate about play. Once a new regime is established there will still need to be termly assembles or group meetings to manage and celebrate the ever-shifting nature of play. Play staff will also have to be skilled in dynamically managing fluid situations during play. These frequent dialogues are necessary because play is not like other activities where outcome and method are fixed. Children need to be able to explore and create in their own way in their play. Fixed rules for everything will never work because play is infinitely variable. The solution is to talk about their play with children as issues arise and as play evolves. Play is practice for life and in life we are much better equipped if we have the skills to identify what kind of situation we are in, make assessments, make judgements and be innovative and resilient rather than having a rule book for every situation.

Parents

Schools should be proud of the quality of their play provision. They should also be professional and self-aware about what their approach is and why they do what they do. Schools should communicate with parents and celebrate how happy good play makes their children, through film, photo and words by newsletter, different media and invitations to 'come and see' what we do.

Great school play environments don't look great to the untrained eye. They tend not to have a wow factor because their aim is to provide many choices and many possibilities for engagement for many children. A well played-in environment will not look pristine, the grass will get worn, the plants will be tatty, there will be mud and lots of objects to move around, and the surfaces may well be chalked on. Parents need to know why the environment looks the way it does, and the best way is to provide regular opportunities and invitations for them to come and join in and play or observe, and for their children to have chances to express their views on the value of their play.

CASE STUDY: ENGAGING PARENTS

One of the OPAL schools in the North East wanted to engage with parents in one of the old pit villages near Durham. They collected lots of loose parts from builders, a garage and parents' donations, and advertised a den-building afternoon with all invited. The turnout was huge with around 60 parents and carers attending and 120 pupils. The parents came to a short talk about the value of play and the reasons behind the emphasis on quality play being part of an excellent school. Everyone then spent the afternoon in a playful session of den building. As the rain became steadily heavier over the afternoon, those with the more stable and waterproof dens reaped their rewards and sheltered the poorer builders. The activity was not completely free play, in that an outcome was set in advance, but the approach and afternoon were very playful and the parents experienced the value of fun, initiative, team working and imagination for themselves.

The play team

It is always surprising in OPAL's work to find out how little management there is to support the staff who provide for the most difficult 20 per cent of school life. Teachers have planning days, training, professional development, observations, results monitoring, etc. Play staff may get a job description and that's it.

A great play offer in schools requires a steady and continuous approach. Children love newness, so play staff need time to research and introduce free or very cheap ideas to keep what's on offer refreshed. To manage ongoing change, both in what they are providing and in how they respond to the constant changes in direction of child-initiated play, staff need timetabled and structured sessions to communicate with each other.

What happens at playtimes is not isolated from what happens in the rest of the school day, and yet the staff may well feel very isolated. Sometimes their names and pictures are not included on the staff board, sometimes they do not feel welcome in the staff room, sometimes – despite years of service – staff do not know their names. Schools need to have a communication plan detailing when and how play staff talk to each other, how they can share information and decisions with the teaching staff and how they are made to feel included and valued. This may be through a noticeboard, a slot in the newsletter, attendance at parts of staff meetings by a representative who provides liaison. Without planning for play-team communication, the school will be likely to develop completely different play cultures for teacher-led play at morning play and supervisor-led play at lunchtimes. The resulting confusion and lack of consistency will have a negative impact on children's behaviour.

The caretaker/grounds staff

The purpose of the caretakers and grounds staff is like every other role in the school, to serve the developmental needs of the children. That is what schools are for. They are not ornamental gardens, wildlife reserves or bowling greens. The people who maintain and care for the physical environment must be aware that the environment cannot be cared for in isolation from its purpose. OPAL has encountered many schools where this is not the case, and somehow the caretaker has the ultimate power of veto over any change to their realm.

Good communication with the caretaker and grounds care staff will help them to understand their role in delivering the school's strategic plan, anticipate any likely problems, and encourage skills and knowledge that can contribute to the play value of the landscape flourishing.

There are many practical details that need to be discussed with grounds care staff during the process of development.

PRACTICAL TIPS

1. *Start right.* Before making changes talk to the grounds care staff to find out what adjustments to plans would make care for them much easier. These discussions should be about how the changes are managed, not whether they take place. Changes may well mean more work, but then everyone's job would be much less work if only the children were kept out.

2. *Make room.* How wide are the mowers – the tractor mower, ride-on and hand. Don't make features just too small to get the mowers between them.

3. *Material migration.* Don't put materials like stones in areas that can easily spread into short grass areas where the mowers will run over them.

4. *Tidy up for the team.* Children should be involved in a complete put away of loose materials before the grounds team come to maintain the area.

5. *Give it a rest.* Children are tough on plants. Teach them not to damage them (especially bark stripping) and give planted areas a year's rest in rotation around the site.

This book returns to the theme of policy and values many times. This is because play is challenging to adults. Its nature is to push back boundaries. If adults are not able to understand, express and share the reasons for their decisions around play, then every challenge will erode the possibilities until only the absolute minimum is provided.

KEY POINTS

» Policy is the way a school expresses its consensus on its values and principles.

» Decisions on play should be founded on policy not fear.

» Turning policy into practice requires lots of ongoing, planned communication.

9

SUPERVISION
From Policing to Playwork

A very significant part of creating lasting improvement to play is changing the perception, the role and the status of the people in charge of one-fifth of primary school time. Playtimes and the people in charge of them are important because play is important, and when they are poorly managed it means there is a huge wasted opportunity for benefits and an increase in problems. The creation of a 'play team' with the right name, job description, clothing, team meetings and celebration of their work and achievements has helped in many schools.

The play team are made up of whoever are the people outside overseeing the majority of play. In the UK this will be a mix of teaching assistants and lunchtime staff. Their job during this time should therefore be focused on meeting children's play needs and creating as rich and diverse a play offer as possible. The profession that does this is called playwork.

The playwork profession has developed over the past 75 years and playwork qualifications can be gained in England at every level from a level 2 basic higher education certificate in playwork through to a bachelor's or master's degree, but surprisingly there has been very limited crossover into schools. OPAL strongly promotes the idea of the role of adults in school playgrounds shifting from a policing role to a playwork role. In policing the job is to stop bad things happening and this is done by presence and prohibition. The suggestion is that by being present and sometimes intervening to stop an argument, behaviour or action, then everyone will get through playtime and the order of the classroom can be returned to. This is not a fun job, especially when many lunchtime staff are virtually excluded from the rest of school life. When the policing model is followed it can be a difficult, cold, demanding and thankless job for staff and lead to constant friction and frustration with children.

The shift to playwork is not about changing the name of the job. OPAL has come across plenty of schools with a policing model and a play worker job title. If staff are to gain satisfaction from their job, their work conditions must meet certain well-researched criteria[16] which include doing good for society, scope for creativity, being valued[17] and having a degree of control (agency). A playwork approach requires a school to understand that the play team are delivering one day a week of the school's offer, and they are responsible for implementing a policy founded on the UN Convention on the Rights of the Child. A playwork approach means the school needs to invest in the playwork team rather than in an occasional capital project with marginal play value. A playworker with a good idea will provide ten times more play value with free or low-cost items than a fixed-use play object.

It can be very difficult for staff to perform different roles in a school. Expecting someone who monitors the dinner hall, where order and quiet are expected, to step outside and become a great playworker is asking for a huge shift in approach. Similarly, asking teaching assistants – who are trained to help deliver teaching outcomes – to foster child-led play is a considerable challenge. The answer lies in appropriate and regular training and in opportunities for team discussion. If staff are aware of the difference between a teaching role and a playwork role, they have a much better chance of being able to provide both.

A very common observation of senior school leadership about their current playtime staff is that they don't do anything, that even when training is provided the benefits don't last, and without teaching staff being present supervisors would rather chat with each other than be active. Once the OPAL programme has started it usually emerges that the word 'play' does not appear anywhere in the job description, training involves being shown where the playground and toilets are, and management, if provided at all, consists of 15 minutes every term for problems to be aired. Great play in schools is above all about the culture of the organisation, what it believes itself to be and how it leads others in its vision. The group of people with the least employed hours, the least training, the lowest levels of qualification, the least power and the lowest status in a school are the very last people to have the confidence and means to change the culture of the organisation.

The single most important thing you can do to make play better

The 200-plus schools to have been through the OPAL Primary Programme all saw the benefits of better playtimes, but while in some the benefits lasted for many years, in others things slowly returned to past patterns. The secret of the ones that lasted was the creation of leadership roles for play. In large schools this included a funded part-time play coordinator post. In small schools it is just another of multiple roles that a staff member takes on. Leaders should lead others to follow the reflective practice cycle:

- What are we trying to achieve? (vision, policy, playwork principles, rights, school mission)

- How well are we doing? (child surveys, play audits, peer observations, team meetings)

- What will we do to improve? (planning, resourcing, relationships, training, practice)

Playwork principles

For over 50 years the playwork sector has specialised in developing a better understanding of what the very delicate, complex relationship should be, between adults and children, in the enrichment of play. The reason for this complexity is a dichotomy at the heart of playwork. If play is about the child's intention, self-direction, ownership of their actions and freedom, what should an adult be doing in play?

Schools can benefit greatly by using the skills, knowledge and principles of the playwork sector in areas of workforce development related to free-play opportunities. The Playwork Principles[18] establish the professional and ethical framework for playwork and as such must be regarded as a whole. They describe what is unique about play and playwork, and provide the playwork perspective for working with children and young people.

They are based on the recognition that children and young people's capacity for positive development will be enhanced if given access to the broadest range of environments and play opportunities:

1. All children and young people need to play. The impulse to play is innate. Play is a biological, psychological and social necessity, and is fundamental to the healthy development and wellbeing of individuals.

2. Play is a process that is freely chosen, personally directed and intrinsically motivated. That is, children and young people determine and control the content and intent of their play, by following their own instincts, ideas and interests, in their own way for their own reasons.

3. The prime focus and essence of playwork is to support and facilitate the play process and this should inform the development of play policy, strategy, training and education.

4. For playworkers, the play process takes precedence and playworkers act as advocates for play when engaging with adult-led agendas.

5. The role of the playworker is to support all children and young people in the creation of a space in which they can play.

6. The playworker's response to children and young people playing is based on a sound up-to-date knowledge of the play process, and reflective practice.

7. Playworkers recognise their own impact on the play space and also the impact of children and young people's play on the playworker.

8. Playworkers choose an intervention style that enables children and young people to extend their play. All playworker intervention must balance risk with the developmental benefit and wellbeing of children.

The purpose of supervision

How many adults do you need to supervise play? The answer to this depends on whether you believe children are able to develop competence and self-regulation or not. When adults are responsible for a large number of children, have minimum training and management, and a brief to keep children safe and manage behaviour, the outcome is likely to be unhappy all round. Either you intervene constantly in play, telling children to 'Get off that', 'Put that down', 'Come away from there' and 'Don't touch' and be subject to growing frustration and hostility from the children; or you stand around trying to let them get on with their play feeling that you are not doing a good job. Problems around supervision are made much worse when staff are not trained and managed in how to form good relationships with children and have a clear behaviour policy to follow. Sadly, shouting, repeatedly picking on one or two children, finger pointing and even rough handling are not uncommon when frustrated lunchtime staff are dealing with difficult playtimes. The solutions are simple: better play will resolve 80 per cent of the issues, and clear support and training to implement a consistent behaviour policy (such as traffic-light cards, time-out areas, or emoticon cards) will deal with the remaining 20 per cent.

The frustrations of the supervisor's job come back to a lack of strategic direction from the school about the purpose of their role and the degree to which the school demonstrates how it values the supervisor's role. As long as the job is framed in negative terms staff are unlikely to feel motivated in their work.

Supervision types

During the development of the OPAL programme within South Gloucestershire Council, it became clear that a greater level of definition of what is meant by supervision was needed. Working with the Schools Health and Safety Officer, three types of supervision were identified.

1. *Direct*: This is when adults need to see what every child is doing at every moment and all children are in relatively close sightline of adults. This would be applicable in situations where there is considerable danger of death or serious injury, it is judged that children have very low levels of competence and where they are unlikely to be able to manage risk or self-regulate behaviour.

2. *Remote*: This applies when adults are visible and reachable by children within the play environment so that they can quickly respond to an accident or incident. The assumption is that every action by every child will not be seen, but that clear processes are in place to deal with incidents should they happen, and that they can quickly be indentified and acted on. It is expected that risk will be controlled by managing the environment and building competence in the children.

3. *Ranging*: This applies on large school sites which might have areas away from open view, such as around corners, over mounds, in woodland or long grass. Supervisors would range over the site so they have an idea of the kind of play going on and where children are. This kind of supervision relies on children being supported in identifying and managing risk, and building self-regulation skills and social skills. This kind of play will take place in an environment where risk–benefit assessments have been made.

These descriptions raise the question: To what degree are staff there to supervise and to what degree are they getting involved and engrossed in their playwork role? The answer is that a good playworker will always keep their 'sixth sense' active. They are able to keep an overview of what is going on and when it is appropriate to respond to a play invitation, help source a needed part, tie a knot or prompt an idea. Good playworkers can never be completely engrossed in the play;

that is the child's job. They must always reserve part of their attention to the awareness of the whole site.

The ability of children to exploit the playfulness of any situation means that even in poor environments staffed by adults who don't understand and don't improve the quality of play, the children will still find ways to be playful. However, their options will be limited, as the potential number of choices in such environments will be much poorer than those in an enriched environment with supportive staff. In these poorer environments, children are much more likely to create play that is challenging to adults, finding their excitement through creating dramatic situations, such as arguments, fights, deliberately getting hurt, crying and spurious first-aid demands. These dramas are intended to draw in adults and so the need for greater supervision is perceived. It is common for schools to comment that they could not possibly cope with enriched play, because even more supervisors would be needed to control all of the new options, whereas universally the opposite is the case and the more options made available the less policing supervision is needed.

CASE STUDY: SUPERVISION LEVELS ARE CULTURAL

I have visited schools in several counties and all of them share the principle that an adult should be present to supervise play. However, how many adults are present and what they are for varies enormously. In Malmö I visited a school situated in a public park. There were no fences or barriers and children could go to play in the park. One adult was in the playground for 250 children. In Canada, where most school grounds double as public open spaces before and after school, and there are no secure boundaries, the ratio is often one adult to a hundred, which is similar to many schools I visited in Scotland. The purpose of this kind of supervision is for children to have an adult available to report concerns to or to respond to incidents, not to be able to police every action of every child. In several UK schools I have visited there have been around 12–14 supervisors, and when I have suggested improvements I have been told that they would not be possible because of lack of supervision.

The overseas models of supervision tend to assume a much greater degree of competency than in the UK. This view of the competent child is also behind the rise in the forest-school approach, which is continuing to grow in popularity. Underpinning this approach is an assumption that a four-year-old can be a capable and competent person, they can remember and follow instructions, use tools and keep themselves within agreed geographical boundaries.

Many English primary schools have improved the quality of their early years' provision but not their whole-school play approach. They use a competent child model, empowering children to become independent and resilient up to the age of five and then undo their good work by withdrawing both enriched play and assumptions of competence at around the age of five-and-a-half.

In larger schools it may be possible to create two separate teams, one for the logistics of meals and one for playwork. This makes sense if there are enough staff because the jobs are so different. Feeding lots of children, in a crowded space, in a short space of time does not require someone trained in self-directed, intrinsically motivated and freely chosen activity. In smaller schools it may be possible to have one person who has a greater playwork role and is the imaginative, resourceful inspirer of a continually evolving play environment.

The presence of adults in a play environment is ultimately both a threat to and an opportunity for the quality of play. The threat comes from lack of skilled intervention, poor relationships between children and adults, and an inability to make good judgement calls on risk–benefit. The opportunity comes from empowering children to improve their judgement skills, enabling appropriate challenge and enrichment of ideas, skills and resources.

KEY POINTS

» Playwork is the profession dedicated to serving children's play needs.

» School playtime staff should have a positive playwork role.

» Playwork puts the child and their play at the centre of all practice.

— 10 —

EQUALITY

Play is a universal right for all children regardless of their age, sex, gender or ability. The idea of equality of access can be difficult to interpret in the context of providing rich, varied and challenging play environments, because what is a challenge for one child might be completely inaccessible to another. For example, a rope walk can be fun and exciting for an able-bodied child but cannot be accessed by a wheelchair user. However, if every part of a play landscape had to be fully accessible to all, the result would be uninspiring and unchallenging for most users. The solution to this problem is to concentrate on whether each child has a rich and varied play offer and whether all children can be integrated with other children throughout the physical environment.

In the case of the rope walk and the wheelchair user it is useful to ask, What is the play offer or experience that the rope walk offers? A child on a rope walk will experience a journey that feels unstable, is above the surrounding ground and feels risky. An inclusive design approach will seek to provide a similar set of experiences for children with different skill or ability levels. An uneven pathway, a wide see-saw or a gentle wobbly bridge might provide a wheelchair user with a similar set of experiences and do so without segregating the children who use them.

Gender bias

Gender bias is almost universal in UK primary playgrounds because of the cultural dominance of football. Within the restricted areas most schools have or use, football means that around 80 per cent of the open space is taken by around

20 per cent of the most dominant boys. Club football develops many skills but playground football is about possession and conflict, and the issues it causes tend to dominate adults' perceptions of what playtimes are all about. As a result, investment, if available, is disproportionately spent on ball courts and sports coaches, while all of the creative, imaginative, social and dramatic players are left literally marginalised and unresourced.

The best resolution is not to ban football but to concentrate on creating a richer play environment. It has been the case in lots of OPAL schools that the play literacy of the older football players is quite low. They just don't have the range of skills and experience to make the most of enriched play environments. It may well be several years before the younger children who are much more play literate work their way through the school that the problem of football dominance subsides.

CASE STUDY: A PLAY-LITERATE SCHOOL

One large primary school in Kingswood, Bristol, has been providing outstanding play opportunities for all its 500 children for over eight years. In talking each year with the head teacher I remember he told me that there was a noticeable difference once the children who had been in their first year when they first began improving play reached the final year. The head was very aware that he now had an entire school of highly play-literate children. Sometimes lots still chose to play football, but they also knew how to play in many other ways, sometimes dressing up, or disappearing into the bushes, or playing with the infants.

Based on many observations, boys tend to dominate space with football or tag, while the kind of play preferred by many girls requires plenty of comfortable semi-enclosed social spaces, performance props and spaces, items for social and dramatic play and lots of chances to hang upside down. It is therefore pretty universal that the typical empty tarmac playground is likely to be gender biased against girls.

Age bias

In one OPAL school the Play Coordinator surveyed the children on their likes and dislikes about play. One recurrent theme was the segregation of children by age. This is standard practice in many schools, which separate reception from infant and infant from junior. The reasons for these practices are usually lost in school mythology. Its persistence continues because 'It is done because that is the way it is done and it must be for a good reason because otherwise we wouldn't be doing it – would we?'

This is a terrible idea – when was segregation anything else? Children love to care for each other, they love to aspire to be like their elders, to have the competence skills and knowledge of bigger children. The idea of age-appropriate play is an adult misperception. Anyone with knowledge of children knows that sometimes an 11-year-old needs to play like a four-year-old and a capable four-year-old can play as competently as an 11-year-old.

Play is the culture of children. It requires skills, insider knowledge, acquired rules and understanding of the cultural knowledge of the landscape passed from older to younger. Play literacy cannot flourish across the artificial rift of age segregation, and those who hold power over children's play and leisure time should always think twice before segregating children who have a right to be together.

PRACTICAL TIP

If the idea of desegregating playtimes seems too daunting, try starting with 'Freedom Fridays' once a week, where the ages are allowed to mix, and go from there.

Ability bias

When adults think of providing better play for children with additional needs, such as wheelchair users, there is often a tendency to think about very expensive specialised equipment such as a wheelchair swing. It is useful to observe other children playing, see what it is that they enjoy and think about how all children could be included in that kind of play. How could a wheelchair user make a den, get to hide in shrubs and bushes, get dirty, take a risk, play out-of-site of an adult, get wet, transport and carry items or throw things. Specialist equipment provides one specific play experience but children of all abilities need to be offered control, choice and the opportunity to explore the boundaries of their normal day-to-day existence.

KEY POINTS

» Every child has the right to a childhood with daily play.

» Adults have a legal and moral duty to uphold children's right to play.

» The right to play means not making assumptions about gender, ability or age but letting children have choice.

— 11 —

USE IT!
Site Access and All-Season Use

This is one of the most important categories that schools can address and is both challenging and rewarding. There are two key concepts that are relevant to this category: access value and free-range children.

Access value by time

Once schools are committed to the concept of play development they are often keen to carry out physical improvements. Sometimes the impetus to address play development comes from the school having plans to spend raised or capital funds on a grounds project. Urban schools may have very limited space, often just their hard-surface playgrounds, but many rural and suburban schools also have access to playing fields. More fortunate schools also have grounds that may include hedgerows, grassy areas and even woodland. The play value that these environments offer is extremely high, as they provide the space to avoid the friction that results from overcrowding, places to explore and discover, social spaces that can be made in woodland and hedgerows, access to natural loose parts such as mud, twigs, leaves, water, grass and stones, and a chance to enjoy the feeling of freedom of playing away from close adult oversight. These experiences are priceless and may well offer a much greater range of play opportunities and much higher play value than capital projects like low-level obstacles that provide a very limited range of play opportunities.

Figure 11.1 illustrates OPAL's experience of how a typical primary school uses its playing field for play over the whole year. Of 365 days, 180 are term days, 30 are in the summer term and 15 are in the summer term when the ground is dry. The phrase 'We use the field in the summer term' usually means dry days in the summer term, which is 4 per cent of the calendar year or 8 per cent of the academic year.

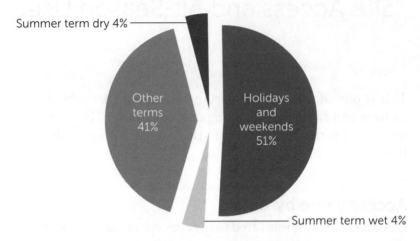

Figure 11.1 School field: Typical annual use

Fields are not used in all weathers because they get slippery, muddy and wet so dirt will get trodden into the school building from shoes and there is a risk of uniform getting dirty or even damaged. An aversion to using fields is understandable, especially in a culture where the benefits of play are not widely acknowledged. Mess and damage will also have an impact on other people, especially caretakers, cleaners and parents. When the value of play is not widely recognised it is logical for the solution to such problems to be the withdrawal of play opportunities. An aim of the OPAL process is to develop a professional community that values highly diverse, rich and plentiful play opportunities. If this is the case, when difficulties are encountered the response from members of the community will be to find solutions that have as little restrictive impact on the children's play opportunities as possible.

The simple message for many schools is 'Look at the true value of what you have already and use it to its fullest possible extent before you invest money in other improvements.'

AN EXERCISE

Work out the value of your existing land. If you are a school lucky enough to have green space, use Google Earth to measure its size, and websites with local property to work out the value.

Access value by space

In places where animals are kept together such as farms and zoos, it is clear that there is a direct relationship between overcrowding and aggressive and anti-social behaviour, and there are no reasons to think that children are any different. Overcrowding in playgrounds triggers stress, creates noise levels higher than allowed in industrial machinery and forces children into conflict. All schools find that that behaviour incidents plummet in the summer term when children are allowed on the field. Just by dispersing children over a wider area, many behaviour issues resolve themselves as children are not constantly forced to make contact with others who they don't want to be with.

AN EXERCISE

Print out an overhead view of the school. Highlight all spaces that could be accessed safely by children for year-round play. Then, highlight areas currently used by all ages all year. Work out the percentage of usable space being used.

CASE STUDY: FROM BATTERY TO FREE RANGE

A school in Devon asked OPAL to help resolve ongoing behaviour problems. We found that each year group was being kept in separate playgrounds and each playground was bleak and overcrowded. The space audit using the exercise above revealed that any individual child was able to access around 7 per cent of the site's usable space in their play. OPAL helped the school do away with all aged-based area restrictions to use all of the spaces between the playgrounds, and use the field and boundary spaces for all of the year. This achieved an increase of 1300 per cent in playable space accessible by any individual child and solved the majority of behaviour issues before we had even addressed improving the quality of the play environment or spent any money.

Free-range children

In the UK there are greater requirements for how much space and time outdoors a free-range chicken should have than a child. The free-range movement has convinced consumers that in order for a chicken to be well balanced, socially adjusted, physically and mentally well, it must have spent at least half of its life outdoors in a good-quality natural environment. Nobody has yet convinced government that children should also have similar standards. In fact, in the UK there is no minimum standard for how much time school children should spend outdoors and no legal minimum requirements for outdoor space in schools. How much space children need in order to be 'free range' we do not know, but we can assume it will be more than a chicken!

In the temperate British climate, for the majority of the time it either looks like it might rain, is raining or has recently rained. In these conditions it is common for children to be driven to school, spend the day in the classroom, have a short time on the tarmac playground and be driven home again. For many children school playtime is the only time they will get to be outdoors playing sociably, and the school grounds may well be the best play environment they are able to access. Schools should be finding every opportunity to get children outdoors and off the tarmac, using their grounds for all of the year. In extreme cases school are managing the best part of the school grounds so that sports day can take place on one afternoon a year.

When a child is left at the school gates, the school takes on the role of guardian. Once a school has created a play policy it may come to realise its guardianship extends beyond care of the child. It is also guardian of the child's time and guardian of the asset of community space. The concept of free-range children rests in the understanding that children have no more power to ensure they are able to access the time, space and freedoms essential for their fundamental wellbeing than the animals that we raise for our food.

All schools should base their decisions about play firmly in policy. In relation to all-weather and seasonal access to their grounds this means that solutions to problems should always be the preferred approach rather than denial of access and opportunity. In practical terms this may mean having to find storage solutions for 200 or more pairs of boots and shoes, resurfacing highly used and easily damaged areas with a more suitable surface or ensuring playtimes are long enough to get changed and to play.

Clothing

The issue of clothing and footwear is one of the most significant in the process of creating the conditions for play. A school's attitude to clothing and footwear and how willing it is to address the issues may be the single most important change it makes in relation to improving the conditions for play. Teachers may come under intense pressure from parents to ensure that shoes are kept clean and unscuffed, and that clothing is spotless and undamaged at all times. In the absence of any agreed policy-based decision on clothing, it is the parents who complain who determine the policy, as important decisions are made in reaction to individual incidents rather than from the basis of agreed values.

The nature of childhood is being changed to suit the demands of children's clothing in and out of school. The function of children's clothing should be to meet the needs of childhood. When a school decides it wants to improve the conditions for play it is useful for them to think about what is the function of the clothing they choose for the children to wear. Different clothing suits different functions. If someone is going to spend the morning at a wedding and the afternoon caving, the hard hat would be more useful than the top hat in the cave, and overalls would be much more practical than a morning suit. The needs of the activity will determine the qualities of the clothing. Good-quality play demands good-quality play clothes, and good-quality play clothes means clothes that allow the child to move freely, to run, to climb, to sit on the ground, to access nature and to occasionally fall over. For many children, both in and out of school, the reverse is true; the quality of play is limited by the qualities of the clothing. This has arisen because parents and teachers expect children's clothing to perform other functions that demand qualities different from playtime clothes and are given precedence.

One of these functions is status. The concept that children are dressed to reflect the income and social status of their parents is not new; it may way be nearly as old as clothing itself. However, the age at which this phenomenon begins and the amount of time in which children are expected to be dressed in clothes unsuitable for play appears to have reached unprecedented levels. Brand awareness is identified in children as young as four. The only possible outcome of this approach to clothing is that the needs of childhood become less important than the needs of the person who determines the clothing. Most primary schools have avoided these pressures by having a school uniform, which removes individual statements about status, and could make it possible for clothing to more fully meet the play needs of the child. Schools, however, frequently use the uniform to replace the individualist statements that parents make about standards and status with their own institutional ones. In these cases the school wishes to link the neatness, smartness and cleanliness of the clothing with qualities of professionalism, status and/or standards. The purpose of the clothing is a marketing message about the perceived standards of the institution to children and to the external world.

If we were truly interested in what is best for children, then the status message of the clothing should be higher the more the clothing meets the needs of the developing child. It is not enough to require boots and coats for four–five-year-olds and then abandon outdoor preparedness. Every child in every schools needs to be equipped to spend extended periods outside all year in play, study and movement. The UK is a mainly damp, rainy and slightly cold climate. It is schools' absolute responsibility to teach children how to live in the climate of their country. Children are currently being kept indoors and sitting down for unhealthy amounts of time. Schools' encouragement of the view that our country is too wet and cold to be outside for all but the finest weather, combined with a lack of all-weather preparedness and other pressures, leads children to view indoor, sedentary consumption of information and entertainment as normal life. This approach is part of an unwitting building of incompetence that happens when decisions are allowed to happen without the guidance of thoughtful policy.

When a school chooses to create a play policy and deliberately improve the fundamental conditions necessary for good-quality play, it can then examine what its priorities are in relation to the function of the clothing. In particular, schools should decide what is the best balance between the statements and qualities the school wishes to promote through clothing and the right of the child to be dressed for the needs of childhood. If the school comes to the conclusion that the two sets of needs are incompatible within one set of clothing, then it needs to develop access to clothing that does enable play to take place. If it decides that both sets of needs are compatible, it may have to adapt the uniform to make it cheaper, more robust, easier to get clean, harder to get dirty or easier to move in. It may also need to work extensively with parents so that the reasons for any changes or applications of policy are understood and supported.

PRACTICAL TIPS

Getting out

Who makes the call? Wet playtimes are often called by the adult who least wants to be outside in the damp. Ensure that it is made by the person who most wants children to be playing outside and that children are kept in only in the most severe conditions.

Footwear

Every child will need a pair of boots, and when they have their boots on they will need a dry place to put their shoes. Investment in well-ventilated covered storage for every pair of boots and shoes will allow at least a 50 per cent increase in use of the school grounds and is money well spent. Schools will have to decide if children bring boots in from home, have to buy a school pair or build their own collection.

Outdoor clothing

Generally, waterproof trousers are not necessary, but it is a good idea to have a number of complete raincoat and trouser sets for children who want to get very wet or muddy in their play. Children should be allowed to bring in old clothes if they wish to get really messy in their play.

Uniform

Uniform needs to suit many needs. Light colours, skirts, ties, pressed trousers and white shirts are smart wear for smart occasions; they are unsuitable dress for early childhood and play.

Storage

Disperse boot and coat storage across the site. Don't cause bottlenecks. Boots are best stored on the boundary between mud and hardstanding, well away from clean entrances. All storage needs to be well ventilated to avoid mould. Young children need somewhere to sit when changing footwear.

Extended access

Over the past 20 years schools in the UK have fenced in playing fields that used to be accessed by children in the community as playable spaces. In other countries, including in Scandinavia, New Zealand, Australia and Canada, school grounds are still regarded as community resources, and in Sweden it is forbidden to fence off most school grounds as they are public spaces.

The reasons for this change vary from school to school and include dogs fouling the grass, vandalism, fear of vandalism, and fears of failing to keep children safe from external risks and threats. Whatever the causes, there are a number of impacts. High fences generally increase children's fear of their community. The message that you are surrounded by people who are a danger to you is well understood by children. The fences have a similar impact on adults who then assume that it is not OK for their children to walk to school because they will be outside the safety of the school's protective fence. A second impact is the loss of amenity space for children. OPAL's analysis shows that once inside the fence, the play field is likely to be played on for around 4 per cent of the year. In areas lacking in other public open space, the play field sitting unused for 96 per cent of the year is a tragic waste and likely to have a negative impact on children's health.

Schools are custodians of a community resource, one that is of immense importance to the quality of childhood and often scarce. When schools invest time and money in improving the conditions for play at playtimes they are also increasing the value of the community asset they hold. In Scotland and Wales there are concerted efforts to get schools to open up and share their community spaces.

Under the Education and Inspections Act 2006, schools in England may also wish to consider their legal duty to promote community cohesion. One of the benefits of good play provision is its positive effect on communities. Parents and carers are able to meet, chat, watch over their children and interact with each other and in a relaxed and playful way, building relationships and bonds that will be carried back out into the community.

Fences do have a positive side when it comes to the kind of play resources than can be left out for children to use in their play. Secure sites can often get away with leaving a lot more loose parts lying around than unsecured sites.

Three of the most common issues that arise from schools seeking to extend access are liability, caretaking and insurance. It may be that the difficulties presented by these issues mean that some forms of extended access – for instance, open use of the grounds at any time for play – are not feasible, but there may be many other lesser steps that still would have great benefits.

PRACTICAL TIPS

- Increase access with an after-school club, especially for free messy play.

- Encourage parents to stay and play for 15 minutes after school.

- Find out what other organisations, for example nurseries or groups such as brownies or cubs, could come and use the grounds for.

KEY POINTS

» Children have a basic need to move around in lots of space and be close to nature.

» Land is a hugely valuable asset and is consistently underused by schools.

» Improving access to land has low cost and high benefit.

— II —

THE ENVIRONMENT OF PLAY DESIGN THEORY

CREATING A LANDSCAPE FOR PLAY IN A SCHOOL

Designing great play environments for schools presents a unique set of challenges. Designers should consider the following:

- *Quantity*: School play environments may well be providing for up to 500 or more children at a time. All of these children will need to find different ways of engaging in their play. So putting in an opportunity such as an outdoor table-tennis table is fun but it will occupy only two, maybe four, children at a time. Children will need many, many different opportunities spread across the site if they are to have their play needs met.

- *Time*: During their time at school, children will be accessing play equipment for around 1,800 hours spread over seven years. As they develop, their environment should not feel stale and worn out but continue to offer them chances for enquiry, stimulation and engagement.

- *Seasonality*: Children will be using a school play environment throughout the year. At home they are not likely to go to the park if it is cold or wet, but at school they will need to get outside for as many playtimes as possible in all seasons and weathers. Choosing surfaces like wet-pour rubber, which gets very slippery in the wet and cold, or having access to grass in winter but no appropriate footwear, will therefore have a huge impact on how much of the school's space is actually usable in changeable climates and seasons.

- *Density*: Many schools have lost, sold, built on or never had enough space for their children. The UK provides better guidance on animal welfare than child welfare in outdoor special standards. Very densely occupied play spaces require especially thoughtful design, so that every intervention has multiple uses, every available space is used, low occupancy equipment does not take up disproportionate space, and space is increased by use of multiple levels and rooftops.

- *Ability range*: The range of children's physical, mental and social abilities from the ages of 4½ to 11 is huge. What must also be considered is that children's play preferences are not linear by age. They like to play up to much older than their age and they like to regress down to early play behaviours, exhibiting a kind of play nostalgia and a desire to relive earlier experience through helping younger children. Schools must also anticipate and provide for the play needs of children with special needs.

- *Site constraints*: Before deciding what should go where, the constraints of the site should be looked at. Where will it be sunny and where will it be cold? Which direction does the wind come from? What is next door? What is the drainage like and what impact will surrounding buildings or plants have on the space?

Adults are inclined to approach design of play environments from a visual, objective and functional approach. They want to know 'what it *is*' and 'what it is *for*'. For instance, 'This is a slide and it is for sliding down', or 'This is a balance beam. It's for walking and balancing along.' This is an outcome-focused approach where we work backwards from knowing that we want children to have the experience of sliding and so we build a slide. In the case of imaginative play we want children to play trains, so we build an object that looks like a train, or we want them to play pirates so we build them an object that looks like a pirate ship.

Children enter a play environment as explorers with no map. They want to explore every aspect of the terrain and discover its every potential for enrichment of their play. The amount of potential for play that any feature possesses has very little to do with what it looks like or what intention an adult has because the nature of play is rooted in the child's intent and the child's desire to be the creative agent behind their own actions. This potential is sometimes called 'affordance' because it refers to the opportunities it affords a child rather than looks or intended function. For example, a hill affords the potential for rolling, sliding, being up high, water flow, hiding, and so on. If the hill was not there, those possibilities could not exist. An environment that affords many possibilities can be said to have high play value. This presents a dilemma for adults wanting to design for play. How do we think up ideas to diversify and improve the quality of play without prescribing and limiting it?

Fortunately children find any elements of difference put into a play landscape afford them a greater number of possible actions, whether intended or not. This is one reason why, however poorly designed a piece of play equipment is, it still provides more difference and therefore play value than nothing. For example, a simple balance beam as a piece of physically challenging play equipment is very time and skill limited. You can walk along it, and if your balance is not very good or developed, it will present playful challenge until you can walk along it, but then the intended function is fulfilled and the object is redundant. However, the object still has some difference and so it can be sat on, jumped over, re-imagined as a crocodile, a bus, etc., used as a safe base for games such as tig or off-ground touch. In terms of value for money the balance beam has provided the same skills development as two tyres and a plank but less versatility. It would be wise therefore that when schools choose to invest in capital fixed equipment they choose the most challenging they can and not the least, as the least can be replicated far more easily with a few free or cheap loose parts.

The testimonies on many play equipment manufactures' websites on the impact of low-level equipment on children's behaviour are much more likely to be about novelty than value. These reactions will have been taken in the first six weeks after opening, when novelty value is at its highest. If you dig several holes in the ground and pile up the soil next to them you will have just as much interest in the first six weeks because of the environmental difference they provide.

In a novel play environment that children visit only occasionally, such as a public park, visual-prompt play equipment can work well as it does not really matter that the range of opportunities for play is quite small, and the prompt to children entering the park that, for example, 'this is for pirate play' can help form a common bond. This is not the case in school grounds. The children know each other and they are in the same environment for 180 days a year for seven years. How much pirate play does a child really want? The day after the child has played pirates they probably have moved on to something else. What other play possibilities will the same features now afford? The pile of rock might be a huge mountain to drive toys cars over. It might be a big cooker to cook the pea gravel food on. It might be a spaceship. The pea gravel might become a family of little mice that live in a cave and explore the mountain. Meanwhile, the pirate ship is always a pirate ship. What is evident is that in terms of play value the rocks are just as good, and probably a lot better in terms of play value for money than the pirate ship, and they cost a lot less.

OPAL's approach to the design of playable landscapes is based on four simple principles. These are universal and applicable in any size space, for any age children and in any cultural context. They are social space, journey, affordance and loose parts, and all need to be present right across a good play landscape.

KEY POINTS

» A school play environment is accessed 180 days a year over several years.

» Children play across a landscape, not on isolated items.

» Only thoughtful and informed design will provide a sustainably engaging environment.

— 13 —

SOCIAL SPACE

If you put a young animal into an open space it will immediately head for the corners and will walk along the edges. As animals we instinctually seek cover and feel more relaxed socialising in enclosed spaces. This behaviour is a deeply engrained survival mechanism and makes sense, because in an environment full of dangers you don't want anything or anyone sneaking up behind you when you are all facing each other socialising.

> **CASE STUDY:** SPOTTING THE
> COSY-SPACE SEEKERS
> On playground observations I always look for children seeking out enclosure of any kind for rest, refuge, observation and socialising. I have found them making a wall out of wheelie bins, jammed between benches and walls, under picnic tables, always in corners and doorways, under bushes, and, when no other cover is to be found, in the toilets. The bleak exposure of the tarmac playground provides literally nowhere to hide, and often children are told to come out of or away from the few refuges they might have found so they can be seen at all times.

Play is primarily but not exclusively a social activity. When asked what they like about play children nearly always say that time to be with friends is very important to them. Social groupings in play vary enormously: children like to play alone, in pairs with their best friend, in small groups of three and four, in medium-size groups of six to ten and in large groups from ten to the whole school. Children are very flexible about these social groupings and are influenced not just by their existing friendship patterns but also by the design of the environment, the resource objects and the nature of the play opportunities on offer.

Social spaces are an essential component of good-quality play and learning spaces. A good social space will draw a group together, encourage interaction, look and feel comfortable and attractive, and provide a set of features that hold or attract the social group so that they want to go to that space and want to stay there. Social spaces work well when they are defined by some form of permeable enclosure. This means that they have a sense of place because they are defined by some enclosing features such as walls, poles, mounding, recessing, planting or fabric but can still be moved through and in and out of in several different ways.

The design of social space should also be social. This sounds obvious, but often seating is provided that prevents social interaction. Isolated benches for two people sitting side by side in an unenclosed place where they are likely to be hit by a football is not as social in design as a horseshoe bench tucked in a place which provides a sense of protection and shelter. A ring seat around a tree trunk means that all of the children must sit with their back to each other, whereas a semi-spiral bench under a tree allows children to choose the extent to which they sit next to or opposite each other. To some degree design can determine behaviour; if you build an attractive shelter that comfortably fits six to eight ten-year-olds, they will find that feature and use it. If you provide little hidey places that just fit two children, then pairs of children will form and use the space. By placing social spaces throughout the whole available environment children can be drawn out to use areas that had previously been sparsely used or ignored.

An important question to ask about any social space is why would you want to spend time there? From an adult perspective we might think about the places we like to go to – our favourite pub or café, place in a park or cinema. We are drawn by a combination of features that include enclosure, comfort, aesthetics, decor, views, activities and sensory stimulation (taste, sounds, imagery). A good social space includes a similar combination of features providing children with fuel for their imagination, sensory experiences, playfulness, invitations to interact with each other or the environment, and opportunities for comfortable rest and engaging activity.

When assessing the quality of the provision of social spaces, we should be looking for an even spread across the whole site of spaces that are suitable for solitary, paired, small-, medium- and large-grouped play. Spaces should have rich and varied combinations of features within them and should above all be well used by children.

The research work of Nilda Cosco[19] demonstrates that when a play environment provides a network of interesting social spaces enriched with a range of playful affordances and this is interconnected by a network of different playful journeys, then levels of movement and interaction are much higher than in open spaces or traditional play equipment environments.

Number

How many social spaces do you need? Children tend to follow a burst–rest pattern in their play. They are active in short bursts, then rest, talk or engage with the surroundings, then move again. The amount of movement is very dependent on the number of interesting place to go. If all the environment is the same, either flat tarmac or flat grass, there is no particular incentive to go to one place rather than another. If there are many places to go and be and each one has its own uniqueness to it then, there are good reasons to go there.

Observations by OPAL suggest that at any time around 60 per cent of children will be in the rest, refuge, socialise and engage phase of play and 40 per cent in movement. This means that for every 100 children around 60 will be seeking a social space. It is helpful to consider provision on this scale as it explains why providing one or two social spaces in a playground is going to lead to overuse, competition and conflict.

Distribution

Social spaces act as a kind of magnet, drawing children to places that would previously not have held an attraction. In order to increase use of the whole school grounds, social spaces should be widely distributed – in singles and clusters – much as the stations on a tube map of London are distributed.

Size

Most social play takes place in pairs and in small groupings, which means there should be lots of attractive small and medium places to go that enclose these groups of children. Occasionally children form together in a group larger than eight, but usually for a game of movement and not socially based play. One or two large gathering places for coming together as a class or team are advisable.

Material

'Found' social spaces can be created anywhere that a space can be demarcated. They work much better when there is vertical enclosure, but can be as basic as a surface change, such as a chalk or painted circle, or a shape mown into the grass. A big favourite is natural enclosure, formed by making a space in the middle of plants, hedges or undergrowth, or deliberately growing plants such as willow, hazel and bamboo to define spaces.

Constructed social spaces can be created in three ways:

1. *Temporary*: Made entirely from loose parts and using fences, walls and anything else that is around to help prop up materials.

2. *Framed*: Uses some permanent designed features to help hold the den up as making a den robust and big enough for groups to get in and play in is challenging in a playtime.

3. *Fixed*: A construction such as a play house, gazebo or outdoor class room that provides a ready-made social space.

Quiet areas

Children may choose to play quietly in some social spaces and they are likely to seek out the most suitable ones if a whole range is provided. Restricting access to a single point of entry and exit will cut down run-through movement; screened enclosure using planting will cut down noise and visual interference; providing comfortable places and surfaces to sit or lie will encourage rest; and providing books, small-world toys or construction will increase the likelihood of quieter play. There is little point in trying to call an area a quiet area and then expending staff efforts trying to enforce quietness.

Quality

It is worth having some spaces that are high quality. These may have an artificial-grass carpet on the floor, attractive colour schemes, pictures on the walls and should be light and clean.

CASE STUDY: DON'T MAKE A
QUIET AREA IN A LOUD AREA

I was observing a playtime in a school where the head had placed a very large outdoor classroom building with three tiers of wooden staging in the middle of the playground and designated it as a quiet area. The children thundered on and off it, running up the three levels and using it as an obstacle to run round, and so one of the three lunchtime staff was positioned next to it to tell children off in a loud voice for not being quiet in the quiet area.

Quiet areas are quiet by location, access and content. Making a rod to beat yourself with and using staff for policing rather than playwork is a dissatisfying experience for everyone involved. If enough choice is provided, children will find the spaces that suit their needs.

PRACTICAL TIPS

- Go for multiples and groupings when making social spaces. Not a playhouse but a play street, not a hut but a village.

- A simple crossbar across two uprights at just the right height for a den is all the structure that is needed to enable a den big enough for several children to be built in a single playtime.

- Rugged native plants (willow for the very short term, hazel and dogwood for the medium term), in big groupings will grow into natural clumps suited to making social spaces.

KEY POINTS

» Enclosed social space is essential for a sense of safety and security in open or busy environments.

» Social encounter is increased in comfortable, engaging social spaces.

» Around 60 per cent of children in a play environment will be seeking a social space.

— 14 —

JOURNEY

A journey in the context of play landscape design is a link between two points. Journeys can be taken using the body in many different ways, such as going under, over, around, climbing, sliding, balancing. We can also think of journeys descriptively: dark, wobbly, squelchy, soft, high, low, etc. Journeys have both a physical and imaginary context in play.

Play has been described as the way in which children come to understand the complexity of their relationship with the world around them. A similar description can be used to describe the function of stories and narrative. We need to feel that our lives make sense, that there is order and reason in the world, and we do this by creating narratives linking events together. In their play, children build playful narratives using their imagination, communication and movement within the physical environment. A good play environment will invite children to move from place to place in many different and exciting ways, drawing them into journeys that become part of the story of their play. This kind of narrative construction play can be heard in younger children as they deliver an ongoing self-commentary about what they are doing and what happens next.

In social–imaginative play children start to join up these narratives, so that instead of lots of individual stories they cooperatively build a common, shared narrative. They use communication to update each other on where the story is going and to negotiate a common view. This story of play develops an ongoing and continuous reaction with the physical world. In fiction and drama the journey is often used as a device to move the plot on. In the world of imaginative play, where the distinctions between reality and imagination become blurred, the physical journey is real but is also simultaneously incorporated into the fictional narrative.

Journeys that are isolated from the other elements of the play landscape will provide much less play value than ones that naturally draw the child from one social space or set of features to another one. An example of this is the wobbly bridge. There are two reasons to play on a wobbly bridge; one is for the physical sensation and challenge of the wobbliness of the bridge, and the other is because the bridge takes you on part of your journey and becomes integrated into the play's narrative. The physical challenge and appeal, as a novel sensation of movement, are likely to be quite shortlived, especially within a school grounds context, as the children will have grown up with access to the feature and will have mastered its physical challenges fairly quickly. The greater play value of the wobbly bridge will be how it can be included in the imaginative and physical journeys around the play landscape. Does it lead from anywhere interesting to anywhere interesting? What does it cross that might make it relevant to the children's imaginative narrative?

Some features built as journeys are used socially by the children as social spaces because they may be the best places available where the children can sit in groups and hang out. This can lead to children blocking the direction of travel for others, especially when all of the features have been set out as a linear trail. This kind of design forces all the possible movement along a set line of play equipment and sets up the possibility of dispute and conflict as there are only two possible directions of movement. The answer is not to set out play environments in simple lines or circuits but in ways that allow multiple directions of movement at the same time.

An effective play environment is made up of a complex network of interconnecting places and journeys. There will be no obvious or predetermined right or wrong way to move about in this environment. The complex network can be described as something similar to the Underground map of London. There are many ways to get from most places to most other places but some quieter areas only have one route. Such a layout has a much greater capacity for movement than either the line or the circle. When children play in a complex network the physical journey becomes a natural and integral part of the movement of their play. This means that features that present a low level of physical challenge and can be easily mastered, such as balance beams and wobbly bridges, have a much more significant role as they become a relevant part of a wider playful landscape.

Children are able to combine elements from the real and imagined world seamlessly in their play. They are able to take their cues from the potential the environment affords them. In this sense children are capable of playing anywhere because they can playfully use their bodies, their imagination and the other people they are with. Even in a totally bare room they will play with language, social norms, rules, roles, sound and texture. This is not grounds for providing poor play environments as the greater the variety and difference of spaces, movements and materials the richer and more engaging the play experiences in that space will be.

PRACTICAL TIPS

- Use existing slopes and gradients to their full potential by adding in different ways of travelling up and down them. Log steps, tyre steps, rock steps, beam walks, zigzags, ramps, ropes or slides.

- Use tunnels to create exciting ways of moving from one space to another. Plastic tunnels do not need to be buried to be fun, laying them through vegetation or planting around them is just as good.

- Use multiples so that several children can go from place to place at the same time, for example twin or triple tunnels or beams, or wide scatters of stepping-stones.

- If you are putting in a willow tunnel, think about what you are connecting to what. Journeys need to be links between places.

- Creating lots of variegation in topography provides many opportunities for going up, down, over, rolling, crossing, etc. Be generous and go for lots of kinds of hills, not just a single one.

- Always try to find out what services lie under the ground before using machinery to dig it up!

- If commercial play equipment is used, make sure it provides as much challenge as possible and enables the kinds of movement that would be hard to create in other ways, e.g. high climbing and upper-body strength movement. Natural landscaping and materials such as tree trunks, rocks and planting can be used to encourage many kinds of movement.

KEY POINTS

» Children want and need to move their bodies in many different ways as they play.

» A good environment will integrate many ways of moving across the landscape.

» A complex network of places to be and journeys between them greatly increases children's movement.

— 15 —

AFFORDANCE, DIFFERENCE AND MATERIAL RICHNESS

Primary education is about firsts. So many first ideas, thoughts, encounters and experiences occur during children's time at their first school. A 'primary' experience can also mean a direct experience. When we touch, smell, carry, move, stand on, lick or jump off an object, we are having primary experience of them. When children play they are not just encountering the world as passive recipients, they are also responding to it. The world has an impact on us and we respond with a flow of thoughts, emotions and feelings. If I am carrying a heavy log, my arms get tired and feel different. I respond by moving faster, having a rest or maybe dropping the log. If I lie on grass I may get damper, more muddy or I may see animals in it or notice how it smells. This cycle of creation, of action, external response from the world and development of a new frame of understanding by the child is the foundation of all play experiences and the foundation of intelligence.

The current generation of children have never seen so much and experienced so little in terms of primary experiences. Children are exposed to many images, both still and moving, but these abstract arrangements of pixels or dyes have no reference points based on active experiential relationships. A play environment should be a material wonderland, where children have a chance to encounter the richness of the natural and constructed world. Such a place will have many kinds of wood, plant, rock, metal, stone, surface, gradient, texture, colour, space, art, sculpture, cultural reference, objects and chances for random and surprise encounter.

CASE STUDY: LOSING SIGHT OF PLAY VALUE

I was called by the staff at a children's centre to discuss what to do about their outdoor area. During the summer holiday the business manager had decided to use some available funding to sort out the early-years outdoor play area. She called in a large national play company and they removed every scrap of nature and put in 50 per cent coloured rubber and 50 per cent artificial turf and five pieces of low-level play equipment. The justification she gave to staff was that it was much cleaner and easier to maintain. This was certainly true but the resulting area had also removed 95 per cent of the richness, diversity, attraction, changeability and value of the space. When the early-years staff returned from holiday and saw their £20,000 'improved' area some were in tears and the head of early years left shortly afterwards. One lesson is that experts in child development and not business managers or sales reps should be responsible for developing outdoor play and learning environments.

A rich play environment will afford children opportunities to blend imagination and physical experience. Through their playfulness children become familiar with the physical world, with its properties and with the relationship between themselves and the world. In imaginative play children use and interpret the physical world to fit with an ever-changing imaginative world. What is relevant from the child's perspective is how the properties of the material world can be interacted with and incorporated in their play. The relationship between the child and the environment in play is never static. The child interprets and uses the environment, then changes the environment either literally or imaginatively, which then gives them a new perspective or set of possibilities. The challenge for adults when creating play spaces is to let go of the idea of creating opportunities where a single type of play will take place, such as a shop or a castle, as these are fixed features whose purpose has been predetermined by adults. What gives much greater value are designed features that are open to adaptation, change and interpretation. This is especially true for school play environments which will be visited every day and so will need to be much more flexible than sites that are visited only occasionally.

Affordance is provided by features in the landscape, a set of possibilities that would be impossible if the feature was absent – for instance, a set of mounds on the tarmac playground or a hill on the grass area which allows for interaction between low and high, on and off, up and over. Almost any addition to a featureless landscape will increase the range of possibilities for play. Rich environments will afford a very varied and flexible range of uses and interactions.

PRACTICAL TIPS

Enrich your material environment with:

- surfaces: rocks, stones, pebbles, grit, gravel, sand, earth, wood chip, planking, paving, brick, mud, grass, water, marsh, round, sharp, smooth, hard, soft, slippery

- gradients: slopes, terraces, steps, slides, holes, trenches, mounds, hillocks, drops, heights

- flora: short grass, long grass, tussocks, meadow, flower beds, herbs, fruit, scrubland, shrubs, undergrowth, woodland, forest, jungle, living constructions, clearings

- fauna: worms, woodlice, earwigs, beetles, birds, hoverflies, dragon flies, ants

- woods (UK): oak, ash, walnut, cherry, lime, larch, cedar, hazel, elder

- metals: zinc, iron, steel, copper, tin, bronze, brass

- rocks: granites, marbles, limestones, chalks, flints, pumice, slates, clay, quartz

- surprises: cupboards, doorways, windows, treasure chests, statues, sculptures.

KEY POINTS

» Most play environments are material deserts of tarmac, short grass and rubber.

» All difference is playable.

» Play environments should be wonderlands of difference and material richness.

— 16 —

CHANGE

'Loose parts' refers to any materials that children can manipulate for playful purposes. The definition comes from the work of Nicholson[20] and the theory proposes that children's ability to play is greatly increased by the provision of materials that they can move, combine, change, alter and manipulate, and that the potential for creativity increases exponentially with the variety of loose parts.

The play value of fabricated loose parts is often in inverse proportion to its monetary value, meaning that the more loose parts cost, the lesser their play value is likely to be. There are several reasons for this. First, a high-value object needs to be carefully looked after because it costs a lot of money to replace. When a child plays with loose parts the value lies in how the object or material can be adapted to be playable in lots of different ways, and how it can be combined with other objects or the environment. The child wants to put the object to the full possible range of uses. This inevitably means that the object can be tested beyond its limits. In other words, the process of playing with loose parts can often lead to them being broken. We can see this when children play with cardboard boxes. Seeing what happens when six of you try to get in the box or what the box is like after a night in the rain is part of the value of the object itself. If loose materials made available to children in their play require constant or frequent intervention from adults to protect the materials, then their play value is lowered and the quality of the children's play will be adversely affected.

Second, high-value objects are also usually designed for a specific purpose; this may be for a sport (for example, a badminton racquet) or for a particular game (such as oversize outdoor chess pieces). The specific nature of these objects dramatically reduces their value as playable loose parts. Children's play is highly complex, changes form rapidly and can be very fluid in its nature, transforming between real and imagined realms in a way that is incomprehensible to adults. Objects that have a single use or function are therefore of much lower value in play. If the object's design is sufficiently robust and adults' attitudes sufficiently flexible, the play value of the object will be increased – for example, the badminton racquet is just not robust enough to stand up to other uses, whereas a cricket bat can serve equally well as a road drill, a guitar or a crocodile.

CASE STUDY: THE START OF PLAYPODS

While working for South Gloucestershire Council I initiated a project bringing together Children's Scrapstore in Bristol and several colleagues in the South West to investigate the impact of mass loose parts on primary playtimes. The research was conducted in ten schools over a two-year period, eventually emerging as The Scrapstore PlayPod action research project. The projects' final independent evaluation report concluded that providing access to plentiful supplies of carefully selected loose parts can dramatically improve children's experiences at playtimes, and demonstrated that when plentiful loose parts are introduced along with a programme of training and support, the benefits included much greater enjoyment of school, increased inclusion and cooperation, and much more imaginative play.[21] Subsequently, other projects around the world bringing mass loose parts into primary playgrounds have had similar findings.[22]

Natural loose parts have a timeless and intuitive appeal to children, regardless of age, sex or ability. When adults are asked about the places they enjoyed playing in most as children, their favourites usually include the beach, woods and streams, and their top activities were building in the sand, damning streams and making dens. The common factor is that these activities are out of doors and involve using available loose resources to alter the environment.

The human race spent its first five million years in completely natural environments, so it is unsurprising that children have an instinctive attraction to the natural world and an ability to use natural resources in their play. Children are remarkably good at adapting anything they find around them to playful uses. Nature provides mud, sand and gravel, pebbles and stones, sticks and twigs, logs and branches, leaves, flowers and fruit, insects and water as the basic ingredients of play.

Addressing access to natural loose parts can be a low-cost and easy first step in improving play for many schools because the resources are often already on site but not being used, and if they need to be brought on site, they are very cheap compared to commercial products. What stands in the way of schools using free or low-cost natural play resources is not the ability or funds to source them but cultural barriers. These often include: not allowing children out of an adult's sight into the woods or bushes, not allowing children to get dirty, worry about using materials as weapons, not allowing children to wear clothes suitable for play and not allowing children to take appropriate risks. These cultural barriers to play are not confined to schools but have become predominant and often unchallenged in English school culture.

CASE STUDY: TIME TO BUILD

Playtimes at one of OPAL's cluster of schools in former mining villages in the North East have undergone a complete transformation. One noticeable change was the engagement of girls in a much greater variety of play types. The day I visited, the head teacher showed me an enormous den, with several rooms, made from many planks, tyres and builders' tarps. She explained that the den had been an ongoing project all week, evolving, growing and improving as the girls learnt better construction techniques and their plans increased in ambition. The head said they were able to do this as they had switched from daily clear-down to a weekly cycle.

PRACTICAL TIPS

Migration

Loose materials (stones, sand, etc.) will inevitably get spread around. When thinking about where they should be sited, always think about what is directly next to them and how migration out of the source area will be managed.

The following tips are worth considering:

- Walls and banks can help contain material around pebble pits or sandpits.

- Don't site loose, hard materials like stones next to short grass where they will wreck mower blades.

- Don't site loose, fine material next to tarmac or hard standing as it makes falls very likely.

- Do create many opportunities for children to sort, sweep, sieve and tidy as part of the play opportunity.

- Put the messiest and dirtiest stuff as far from indoors as practical.

General storage

The more children can access what they need, where they need it and are able to put items back in a clear and easy way, the less work for adults and the greater opportunities for self-directed play.

It is OK to have two kinds of storage:

- *tidy, clear, and labelled*: picture-labelled boxes, shelves, outdoor cupboards, wall clips, great for tools, forest school resources and outdoor learning materials

- *chuck storage*: big doors, big boxes, minimal sorting, ideal for speedy ends to playtime clearing, and for rummaging for random scrap and junk objects.

Leaving up or taking down?

Many OPAL schools have huge amounts of man-made loose parts available for all children to play with at every playtime. The question always arises about what should happen to the dens and constructions at the end of playtime. Here are some options:

- Everyone picks up three objects and chucks them in the store, whether they have played with them or not.

- Dens are left up all week and Friday is a big clear-down day.

- Wet loose parts stay out. Dry loose parts go away.

- Monitor teams help play staff clear and tidy.

- Poor clear-up one day means no loose parts the next.

Loose parts storage

For storing loose parts, big, well-sited, sufficient storage is essential. The following tips are based on the experience of many schools.

- You can't go too big but will probably go too small.

- Don't choose long and narrow. The access doors should take up 75 per cent to 95 per cent of the longest side of the storage.

- Don't have lots of fussy shelves and boxes. A few big stalls work better.

- In large grounds, consider having multiple units spread around the school site.

- Use the back half of the space for big storage stalls and the front half for big pull-out bins and trolleys.

- Locate storage on routes children will be taking as they return indoors.

Sourcing

The process of a child taking single elements from their play environment and combining them in their own original and creative way is called combinatory play. It is liberating to realise that children get much more play value from combining and exploring random stuff than from carefully selected toys or games. Einstein is quoted as saying that combinatory play is the foundation of human intelligence. Sourcing the plentiful and diverse materials needed for combinatory play requires time and effort but pays amazing dividends in impact. All items should be assessed for their safety and suitability by staff before being given to children.

Items might include:

- *building materials*: pipes, gutters, utility pipes and ducts, off-cuts from planks, insulation, tarps, thick ropes

- *domestic materials*: pots, pans, trays, handbags, clothes, sheets, ladles, spoons, hats, shoes, keyboards, sinks, tables, cupboards, suitcases, briefcases, cuddly toys

- *school materials*: tables, chairs, keyboards, anything that was going to go in the skip.

Looking after the loose parts, removing damaged ones and sourcing an ongoing cycle of replacements requires a deliberate plan. It will not just happen and will certainly not be sustainable without a 'curator of loose parts'. Sources will include items that the school previously threw away and items from staff and parents. It is worth getting together a list of parents who are likely to be able to help, such as tradespeople, builders, suppliers, gardeners, landscape and maintenance workers, utility workers.

Termly appeals, use of pester power from children, visible collection boxes and family play days can all help keep a steady flow of resources coming into the school.

Safety note

The biggest risk to children in play is the risk from looped ropes tied at height. These tips will help keep children safe:

- Don't use very thin twine, string or wire in a school play environment.

- Go for thicker rope rather than thin.

- Never tie any ropes at height on play equipment.

- Keep rope play in areas that are directly supervised.

- Have a worst-case scenario plan.

- Teach children how to think about safety and how to look after the safety of others.

KEY POINTS

» Loose parts enable children to move, change, transport and combine materials and items.

» Loose parts provide the highest value-to-play ratio of any investment in play.

» All and every part of a play environment should include access to natural and man-made loose parts.

CONCLUSION

The rewards to schools of becoming places of wonderful play are so universal, so repeatable and so widespread that improving the quality of play in schools should be a national priority and not left to each head teacher to discover and reinvent for themselves. In Wales and Scotland, national governments have woken up to the importance of addressing a strategic approach to play in schools, from the perspective of human rights, child wellbeing, a whole-child approach to development and providing schools that work better for everyone in them. There cannot be a school in the country that would not love to have happier children, more effective teaching, more skilled, social and healthier children, and the majority of behaviour problems arsing from playtimes disappear.

The United Nations recognises the impact and extent of loss of the habitat of play from childhood in nearly all developed and developing countries, and through their General Comment 17 have reminded member states of their legal and moral obligations to take play seriously. In the UK, the All-Party Parliamentary Group on a Fit and Healthy Childhood[23] also drew attention to the need for concerted action to address loss of play and urged schools to do more.

The accidental loss of play from childhood will not accidentally reappear. Only deliberate and consistent action can now make a difference as the habitat of play will not replace itself.

While national action is desirable, there is a current generation of children who cannot afford to wait for politicians. Schools are in a unique position to make a significant difference to the quality of a nation's children, at the same time as gaining significant benefits to themselves. Delivering this difference requires a deep understanding of the nature and benefits of play, and a commitment to change the culture and values of the whole school community. This cultural shift is not easy and some may not be prepared to go through with it, because ultimately play requires us to trust that children are competent and capable and that they are able to learn, regulate their behaviour and think without constant adult direction and intervention.

The emphasis in this book has deliberately been on the ideas and structures that support sustainable cultural change, as it is only once these are secure that it makes any sense to address the environment. The 16 years of action research behind OPAL's work has repeatedly proven that schools that understand the nature of play as freely chosen, self-directed, intrinsically motivated behaviour and provide clear leadership roles, policy documentation, forward planning, ongoing resourcing and support a playwork approach in their staff, will become and remain great providers of play, whatever the limitations of their physical environment. In contrast, many schools pour huge amounts of money into the physical play environment while ignoring the cultural conditions, and find only brief and marginal benefits, not the transformational change they were hoping for. Just as play is a process not an activity or set of activities, so play development is a process. It is certainly not something someone comes and builds for you in a couple of weeks.

The work to make a school a great provider of play opportunities for all its children is considerable, but the rewards are beyond doubt more than worth the effort. They have been described as 'transformational' by many heads, with the impact reaching far beyond the playground, into the classroom and the entire character of the school itself.

The final word should be left to a head teacher.

OPAL has revolutionised our play at lunchtime. From being football dominated, we now offer an exciting, creative, physical environment which has something to offer everyone. Children are now highly active and interactive, challenged both physically and mentally. There is high-quality role-play, greater integration across the school and so much creativity. You can build a den, play in the mud kitchen, chat in the stilt houses, swing on the tyre swings, enjoy a picnic, dig to your heart's content – the possibilities are endless and our children love it. (K. Hemmings, Head Teacher, Tanfield Lea Primary School)

NOTES

1. Bath and North East Somerset Council Play Policy, 2000.
2. OFCOM (2016) *Children and Parents: Media Use and Attitudes Report 2016*. Available at www.ofcom.org.uk/research-and-data/media-literacy-research/children/children-parents-nov16, accessed on 11 January 2017.
3. OECD (2014) 'Does homework perpetuate inequities in education?' *PISA in Focus 46*. Available at http://www.oecd-ilibrary.org/education/does-homework-perpetuate-inequities-in-education_5jxrhqhtx2xt-en, accessed on 7 December 2016.
4. Press Association (2016) 'Children spend only half as much time playing outside as their parents did.' *The Guardian*, 27 July. Available at www.theguardian.com/environment/2016/jul/27/children-spend-only-half-the-time-playing-outside-as-their-parents-did, accessed on 7 December 2016.
5. Carter, C. (2014) 'Children spend less than 30 minutes playing outside a week.' *The Telegraph*, 6 April. Available at www.telegraph.co.uk/lifestyle/10747841/Children-spend-less-than-30-minutes-playing-outside-a-week.html, accessed on 7 December 2016.
6. Blatchford, P. and Baines, E. (2006) *A Follow-Up National Survey of Breaktimes in Primary and Secondary Schools: Final Report*. London: The Nuffield Foundation.
7. Carter, C. (2014) 'Children spend less than 30 minutes playing outside a week.' *The Telegraph*, 6 April. Available at www.telegraph.co.uk/lifestyle/10747841/Children-spend-less-than-30-minutes-playing-outside-a-week.html, accessed on 7 December 2016.
8. United Nations (1989) *Convention on the Rights of The Child*. Available at www.unicef.org.uk/what-we-do/un-convention-child-rights, accessed on 7 December 2016.
9. Available at www.iccp-play.org/documents/news/UNGC17.pdf, accessed on 5 December 2016, p.3.
10. Committee on the Rights of the Child, General comment No.17. Available at www.iccp-play.org/documents/news/UNGC17.pdf, accessed on 5 December 2016, pp.21–22.
11. Ball, D., Gill, T. and Spiegal, B. (2012) *Managing Risk in Play Provision: Implementation Guide*. London: National Children's Bureau. Available at www.playengland.org.uk/media/172644/managing-risk-in-play-provision.pdf, accessed on 7 December 2016.
12. See note 11.
13. Health and Safety Executive (2012) *Children's Play and Leisure: Promoting a Balanced Approach*. Available at www.hse.gov.uk/entertainment/childrens-play-july-2012.pdf, accessed on 5 December 2016.
14. See note 11.
15. See note 13.
16. *The Guardian*, 'What makes us Happy at Work', 11 June 2014
17. Matta, C. (2015) 'Why It's Important to Feel Valued At Your Job.' Available at http://psychcentral.com/blog/archives/2012/10/09/why-its-important-to-feel-valued-at-your-job, accessed on 10 January 2017.

18. The Principles Scrutiny Group (2004) 'The playwork principles.' Available at www.playwales.org.uk/eng/scrutinygroup, accessed on 6 December 2016.

19. Cosco, N.G., Moore, R.C. and Islam, M.Z. (2010) 'Behavior mapping: A method for linking preschool physical activity and outdoor design.' *Medicine & Science in Sports & Exercise 42*, 3, 513–519. Available at https://naturalearning.org/sites/default/files/Cosco_Moore_Islam_BehaviorMapping.pdf, accessed on 7 December 2016.

20. Nicholson, S. (1971) 'How not to cheat children: The theory of loose parts.' *Landscape Architecture 62*, 30–34.

21. Armitage, M. (2010) *Play Pods in Schools: An Independent Evaluation (2006–2009).* Available at www.yapaka.be/sites/yapaka.be/files/page/rapport_independant_mene_en_angleterre.pdf, accessed on 7 December 2016.

22. Hyndman, B.P., Benson, A.C., Ullah, S. amd Telford, A. (2014) 'Evaluating the effects of the Lunchtime Enjoyment Activity and Play (LEAP) school playground intervention on children's quality of life, enjoyment and participation in physical activity.' *BMC Public Health 14*, 164. Available at http://bmcpublichealth.biomedcentral.com/articles/10.1186/1471-2458-14-164, accessed on 7 December 2016.

23. APPG (2015) *Play: A Report by the All-Party Parliamentary Group on a Fit and Healthy Childhood.* London; APPG. Available at www.royalpa.co.uk/?p=the_appg_on_a_fit_and_healthy_childhood, accessed on 7 December 2016.

INDEX